ISBN:979-8-9922475-5-8

This book is intended as a practical resource and informa-
tional guide. It is not a substitute for professional counsel-
ing or therapy. The author and publisher assume no liabil-
ity for outcomes related to the use of this book.

The Science of Letting Go

Mastering Surrender in a World of Control

by

Ethan Starke

Preface

There comes a point in every life when the weight of control becomes unbearable. When the carefully constructed plans, the tireless efforts to shape reality to our will, and the unrelenting need for certainty all begin to crumble. For me, that moment was not a single event, but a series of unravelings—losses that stripped away my illusions, failures that forced me to question everything I thought I knew, and moments of surrender that, against all logic, led to my greatest transformations.

This book is not about resignation. It is about liberation. It is about the paradox that life teaches us again and again: that true strength is not in grasping, but in letting go. That surrender is not about giving up—it is about stepping into something greater.

I did not come to these realizations easily. I fought them. I resisted. I spent years believing that security came from control, that success was the result of unrelenting effort, and that identity was something to be meticulously built and fiercely defended. But life, in its wisdom, had other plans. Through financial collapse, heartbreak, personal reinvention, and spiritual awakening, I was forced to confront the very thing I feared most—uncertainty. And in doing so, I discovered a truth far more powerful than any plan I could have devised: that when we stop clinging, life moves through us in ways we never could have imagined.

This book is a guide to that process of surrender—not as a passive act, but as an active, intentional way of living. It is rooted in personal experience, but also in psychology, philosophy, spirituality, and the wisdom of those who have walked this path before. It explores the fear of letting go, the resistance we feel when faced with change, and the quiet, profound transformation that happens when we release our grip and trust what is unfolding.

If you are reading this, you may already feel the tension between control and surrender in your own life. Perhaps you are at a crossroads, standing on the precipice of an ending you didn't expect or a beginning you're not sure you're ready for. Perhaps you are clinging to something—a belief, a relationship, an identity—that no longer serves you, but the idea of letting it go feels terrifying.

I understand that fear. I have lived it. And I also know what lies beyond it.

Letting go is not the end of something. It is the beginning of something else—something wider, freer, more expansive than we ever imagined.

This book is an invitation. To loosen your grip. To trust the process. To step into the unknown—not with fear, but with the quiet, unshakable knowing that you are exactly where you need to be.

Because life has a way of catching us when we finally stop trying to hold it all together.

And in that moment, we discover what surrender was always meant to be: not loss, but freedom.

Ethan Starke

Introduction: The Paradox of Control

We live in a world where control is celebrated as the ultimate virtue. We're told to map out our lives meticulously, to perfect every detail, and to manage uncertainty with unyielding resolve. This narrative promises safety, success, and fulfillment. But does it deliver? For many of us, the pursuit of control creates a different reality—one of anxiety, stress, and perpetual dissatisfaction.

Take a moment to reflect on the last time life threw something unexpected your way. Did you scramble to regain control, only to feel the weight of fear and frustration settle deeper into your chest? Or did you pause and let yourself adapt to the uncertainty, trusting in your ability to navigate whatever came next?

The science behind our need for control is rooted deep in our biology. When faced with uncertainty, the brain activates the amygdala, the region responsible for processing fear. This triggers the release of stress hormones like cortisol and adrenaline, putting us into a heightened state of alert. While this response evolved to protect us from immediate physical threats—like a predator in the wild—it's far less helpful when the "threat" is a missed deadline, a financial setback, or an unexpected life change.

In today's world, uncertainty is constant. Yet our biological response hasn't evolved to match this modern reality. Instead, it often works against us, leaving us stuck in cycles of overthinking and anxiety. Neuroscientists have found that prolonged uncertainty can override the brain's prefrontal cortex—the region responsible for rational thinking—making it harder to process challenges calmly or creatively. This explains why, under stress, we often cling to rigid plans or micromanage situations, even when doing so increases our frustration.

The irony is that our efforts to control often backfire. Research published in Nature Neuroscience shows that individuals who habitually seek control over uncertain situations report higher levels of stress and lower overall well-being. Conversely, those who practice letting go—through techniques like mindfulness—experience reduced amygdala activity and greater emotional resilience.

So, what does this mean for us? It means that the key to navigating life's uncertainties isn't found in grasping tighter but in learning to release the grip. It means retraining our brains to see uncertainty not as a threat, but as an opportunity for growth.

This book isn't about abandoning ambition or giving up on the life you want. It's about discovering a new way forward—a way that embraces surrender, not as defeat, but as liberation. Surrendering doesn't mean relinquishing your agency; it means choosing to release the illusion of control over what you cannot change while focusing on what truly matters: your mindset, your choices, and your capacity to adapt.

Control didn't just enter my life as an adult—it was ingrained in me from childhood. My father was a man of high expectations and precise standards. Perfection wasn't just encouraged; it was demanded.

I remember one moment vividly, a routine occurrence that became insignificant at the time though it always felt unnatural and stress inducing. My father would ask me to bring him cold drinking water. Simple enough, right? But in my house, even the smallest tasks carried an invisible checklist. The water had to be cold, not room temperature, but not cold that it would hurt my father's sensitive throat. The pitcher had to be full, but not too full. I had to deliver it quickly, but not run. I had to stand in just the right spot to hand it over and wait for him to finish before retrieving it.

Any misstep was met with a verbal lash and sometimes just a look—not anger, but disappointment, which somehow felt worse.

That moment encapsulates my childhood: a series of tests where the goalposts were always moving. An "A" on a report card was good, but why not an "A+"? Completing today's chores was expected, but why not finish tomorrow's too? Play was indulgent; work was virtuous. Surrender wasn't an option—it was weakness.

By the time I was ten, I had internalized the lesson: control everything, or risk failure. What I didn't realize was how deeply that belief would shape my life—and how much it would cost me.

Fast forward to September 20, 2006. I had just quit my job in Dubai to start my first company, moved to Abu Dhabi, and begun living with Javier, my first boyfriend, who had relocated from Madrid. It should have been a time of excitement and possibility, but instead, it felt like a storm I couldn't contain.

The business wasn't taking off. Money was running out. Javier, far from home and dependent on me for everything, was struggling to adjust. And I was trying to manage it all—relationships, finances, dreams—with the same iron grip I had learned as a child.

That day, Javier said the words I wasn't prepared to hear: "I think we need a break. Let's try to be friends."

I was paralyzed. My instinct was to fix it, to control the conversation, to make him see how much I was doing. But I couldn't. For the first time, my grip on life felt completely useless. I watched helplessly as he walked out the door, taking with him the plans we had made for Christmas, New Year's, and a summer wedding in Ibiza.

Looking back, I can see it clearly. My need to control everything—my business, my finances, even Javier's happiness—had driven a wedge between us. But at the time, I couldn't admit that. I blamed everyone else: my cofounder for leaving me to carry the business, my attorney for delays, even Javier for being "too dependent." The truth was harder to face: my need for control had cost me what mattered most.

The lesson I failed to learn in 2006 hit me again, harder, in October 2019. By then, I was at the peak of my career, confident in my ability to control not just my life but the world around me. Lebanon, my home country, was on the brink of financial collapse. My sister came to me, worried about the safety of her savings. "What do you think I should do?" she asked.

I dismissed her concerns without hesitation. "The banks are in control," I said. "Everything will be fine."

She didn't listen. Within 48 hours, she had withdrawn her money and invested it in real estate. I, on the other hand, lost everything. My life savings were wiped out.

That wasn't just a financial loss—it was an identity crisis. My sense of self had been built on the illusion of control. When that illusion shattered, I was left with nothing but questions: Who was I without my achievements? What did I have if not the ability to control my life?

The months that followed were some of the darkest of my life. At the age of 42, I was forced to emigrate to start all over, ended up in Houston, Texas, a city I had no one in where I experienced homelessness, losing my security and my sense of direction. But in that darkness, I found the first glimmer of a new truth: control is an illusion, and letting go isn't weakness—it's survival.

Why Letting Go Matters

Letting go isn't easy. It's counterintuitive, even frightening. Our brains are wired to resist it, and society tells us we shouldn't. We're bombarded with messages that glorify control: Hustle harder. Perfect your routine. Plan your five-year trajectory.

But what if those messages are wrong? What if the key to a fulfilling life isn't control, but surrender?

Neuroscience offers an answer. Studies show that when we release the need for certainty, we activate the brain's "default mode network," which is associated with creativity, problem-solving, and resilience. Research shows that our brains are remarkably adaptable through a process known as neuroplasticity. By practicing mindfulness and releasing the need for certainty, we can reduce the overactivity of the amygdala, the brain's alarm system, and foster a sense of calm even in the face of uncertainty. This rewiring helps us respond to life's challenges with greater clarity and re-silience, opening the door to creativity and problem-solv-ing. Letting go doesn't just reduce stress—it opens doors to possibilities we never imagined.

This book is about that journey. It's about unlearning the habits and beliefs that keep us trapped in cycles of control and embracing a new way of living. This book is your roadmap for transformation. Through each chapter, you'll learn to identify the hidden habits and beliefs that keep you stuck, practice techniques to reduce anxiety and foster peace, and adopt a mindset that embraces flexibility and growth. Whether you're facing professional challenges, personal struggles, or the chaos of everyday life, the tools in this book will empower you to thrive. Through stories, re-search, and practical tools, I'll show you how to let go of what you can't control and focus on what you can: your mindset, your actions, and your capacity to adapt.

A New Way Forward

As Rumi once said, "Try not to resist the changes that come your way. Instead, let life live through you. And do not worry that your life is turning upside down. How do you know that the side you are used to is better than the one to come?"

Letting go doesn't mean giving up—it means making space for what's possible. It means trusting yourself, embracing uncertainty, and finding freedom in the chaos of life.

In the chapters ahead, we'll explore the roots of control, the costs of holding on, and the transformative power of surrender. This isn't just a book about surviving—it's a book about thriving. Because life isn't something you control—it's something you experience. And when you let go, you'll find it's far more beautiful than you ever imagined. When you let go, you step into a world of possibilities. You'll discover a life that's richer, more meaningful, and full of unexpected joys. It's not about giving up—it's about gaining everything you didn't know you were missing.

Chapter 1: Why We Hold On

Control often feels like a shield against the chaos of life. We hold on tightly—planning, organizing, and striving—believing that if we can manage every detail, we can avoid failure, pain, or uncertainty. But beneath this relentless pursuit lies a deeper question: Why do we feel the need to control in the first place?

The answer begins with the human brain. Neuroscientists have long studied how the amygdala, our brain's fear center, reacts to uncertainty. When faced with ambiguity, the amygdala signals potential threats, triggering a stress response that floods the body with cortisol and adrenaline. This mechanism, designed to protect us in life-or-death situations, also kicks in when we perceive everyday uncertainties—whether it's an unpredictable work project or a conversation that didn't go as planned. Over time, this physiological reaction can create a cycle: the more we fear uncertainty, the more we try to control, and the more stress we feel when control proves impossible.

Our upbringing and societal pressures only amplify this cycle. Many of us grow up in environments where achievement is celebrated, and failure is frowned upon. We internalize messages that perfection is the standard, and anything less is unacceptable. These lessons shape our adult lives, leading us to equate control with safety and success.

Take, for instance, the phenomenon of perfectionism—a trait that is often admired but carries a hidden cost. Perfectionists strive for flawless execution, but this pursuit is rarely satisfying. Instead, it leads to chronic stress, burnout, and a constant sense of inadequacy. Studies show that perfectionism is on the rise, driven in part by societal norms that glorify unattainable ideals. Social media, with its curated images and highlight reels, adds fuel to the fire, making it harder than ever to accept imperfection in ourselves or our lives.

The costs of control extend beyond the individual. In relationships, the need to manage outcomes can create tension and disconnection. Partners feel stifled, friendships become strained, and the joy of shared moments is overshadowed by unrealistic expectations. On a broader scale, our collective obsession with control impacts workplaces, communities, and even global systems, leading to inefficiency, distrust, and missed opportunities for growth.

In this chapter, we'll explore the psychological roots of control, uncovering the fears and beliefs that drive it. We'll examine the neuroscience behind our reactions to uncertainty, understanding why letting go feels so difficult—and so necessary. Finally, we'll reveal the hidden costs of control, from emotional and physical tolls to its impact on our relationships and creativity.

By the end of this chapter, you'll not only understand why we hold on so tightly but also begin to see the cracks in the foundation of control. These cracks are not flaws—they are invitations to let go. Because the truth is, control is not the solution we've been taught to believe it is. It's a barrier that keeps us from living fully, loving deeply, and embracing the beautiful uncertainty of life.

Psychological Roots of Control

Fear and Anxiety

At its core, the need for control often stems from fear and anxiety. These emotions, while deeply human, are also deeply uncomfortable. Fear whispers that something could go wrong, and anxiety magnifies that whisper into a roar. Together, they create a powerful drive to manage every detail, anticipate every outcome, and leave no room for error. Control becomes our shield, a way to keep the chaos of life at bay—or so we think.

This need to control is a survival mechanism rooted in our evolutionary history. For our ancestors, uncertainty often meant danger. The rustle of leaves could signal a predator, and an unpredictable food supply could spell disaster. To protect themselves, early humans developed a heightened sensitivity to potential threats, driving them to seek certainty wherever possible. This instinct ensured their survival. Yet the world we live in today is vastly different. Most of our modern uncertainties—missed deadlines, awkward conversations, fluctuating finances—don't threaten our lives. However, our brains haven't evolved to distinguish between a looming deadline and a lurking predator. The same fight-or-flight response that kept our ancestors alive now triggers when we face everyday challenges.

This response originates in the amygdala, the brain's fear center. When we encounter uncertainty, the amygdala sends out an alarm, flooding our bodies with stress hormones like cortisol and adrenaline. These hormones heighten our awareness and prepare us to react quickly. While this can be helpful in emergencies, it's less useful when the "threat" is an uncertain job promotion or an unreturned text. Over time, chronic activation of this stress response wears us down, leading to burnout, anxiety disorders, and even physical health issues like hypertension or weakened immunity.

Fear is particularly insidious because it often operates beneath the surface. On the outside, we might appear driven, diligent, or detail-oriented. We might tell ourselves—and others—that we're simply striving for excellence or doing what's necessary to succeed. But if we dig deeper, we often find that this behavior is fueled by fear. Fear of failure. Fear of rejection. Fear of not being enough. Anxiety then compounds this fear, convincing us that if we don't control every variable, something catastrophic will happen.

Take perfectionism, for example. At first glance, perfection-ism might seem like a positive trait—a commitment to do-ing our best. But for many, the drive to be perfect is less about achieving greatness and more about avoiding criti-cism or judgment. The perfectionist believes that if they can get everything right, they can shield themselves from the pain of failure or disapproval. Yet perfection is an im-possible standard, and the pursuit of it is exhausting. Each small mistake or perceived flaw becomes a source of over-whelming anxiety, reinforcing the belief that they must work even harder to maintain control. The result is a vicious cy-cle: the more they strive, the more anxious they become about falling short. And when they inevitably do fall short, the anxiety intensifies, and the cycle starts again.

This cycle isn't confined to the individual—it ripples out-ward, affecting relationships, work environments, and com-munities. When fear and anxiety dominate our decisions, they shape how we interact with the world. We might avoid risks, fearing what others will think if we fail. We might mi-cromanage those around us, trying to control their actions to ease our own discomfort. In relationships, this often manifests as tension and disconnection. A partner or friend may feel stifled by our need to control, leading to resent-ment and a breakdown in communication. Over time, fear-driven behaviors can isolate us, eroding the very support systems we need to thrive.

Yet fear and anxiety, for all their power, are not insur-mountable. The first step to breaking free is understanding their roots. When we recognize that our drive for control is a response to these emotions, we can begin to challenge the underlying beliefs that fuel them. We can ask our-selves: What am I truly afraid of? What's the worst that could happen if I let go? These questions, though simple, are profound. They force us to confront the stories we tell ourselves—the narratives that keep us trapped in cycles of control.

For many, the answers to these questions reveal a surprising truth: most of what we fear is either unlikely to happen or less catastrophic than we imagine. The fear of failure, for example, often loses its grip when we consider that failure is not an end but a step in the learning process. The fear of rejection softens when we remember that no single person's opinion defines our worth. And the fear of uncertainty becomes less paralyzing when we realize that life has always been uncertain, yet we've navigated it so far.

This understanding paves the way for a crucial realization: while fear and anxiety light the spark, perfectionism and societal pressures fan the flames. These external influences reinforce our need for control, creating an environment where letting go feels not just difficult, but impossible. To truly break free, we must look beyond our internal fears and examine how the world around us shapes our beliefs

Perfectionism and Societal Pressures

Our culture celebrates perfectionism. From a young age, we are conditioned to strive for flawless results—straight A's, the perfect career trajectory, the ideal body. Social media magnifies this pressure, bombarding us with curated glimpses of seemingly perfect lives. It's no surprise that perfectionism has been linked to increased levels of stress, anxiety, and depression.

Growing up, I saw this first hand in my father. A successful businessman, he was the embodiment of perfectionism and control. His achievements weren't just personal milestones—they were standards for everyone around him. To him, success was the product of relentless hard work, meticulous attention to detail, and an unwavering commitment to staying in control. Luck, collaboration, or external factors had no place in his worldview.

As a child, I absorbed this philosophy. My father's voice became the voice in my head, urging me to push harder, to achieve more, to control every aspect of my environment. But this pursuit of perfection came at a cost. Studies show that individuals who internalize high parental expectations are more likely to struggle with self-esteem issues and a fear of failure later in life. These pressures can trap us in a cycle of chasing impossible standards, leaving little room for self-compassion or acceptance.

The societal obsession with perfectionism is particularly evident in our work culture. In the era of "hustle harder" and "no excuses," we are encouraged to overwork, to view rest as laziness, and to equate our worth with our productivity. Yet research reveals the dangers of this mindset. Perfectionists are more likely to experience burnout, reduced productivity, and a diminished sense of fulfillment.

Reflecting on my own journey, I see how perfectionism shaped my early choices. I believed that if I worked hard enough, planned meticulously enough, and controlled every detail, I could avoid failure. But life doesn't work that way. The need for perfection is not only unattainable—it's unsustainable. Letting go of perfectionism doesn't mean abandoning ambition. It means recognizing that our worth isn't tied to flawless outcomes and that true growth often comes from our mistakes.

Where does this relentless pursuit of perfection come from? For many, it begins in childhood. Psychologist Thomas Curran, a leading researcher on perfectionism, has found that parental expectations are a significant predictor of perfectionist tendencies. In his landmark study published in *Psychological Bulletin*, Curran and his co-author Andrew Hill discovered that socially prescribed perfectionism—the belief that others expect you to be perfect—has risen dramatically in the past three decades. This form of perfectionism is particularly damaging, as it fosters feelings of inadequacy, anxiety, and a constant fear of judgment. For children growing up in environments where praise is conditional—tied to achievements like good grades or athletic success—the seeds of perfectionism are often sown early.

But perfectionism is not only a personal battle—it's a societal phenomenon. Social media has amplified this pressure to an unprecedented degree. According to a study published in the *Journal of Social and Clinical Psychology*, individuals who spend more time on social media platforms like Instagram and Facebook are more likely to compare themselves to others, leading to higher levels of perfectionism and depressive symptoms. Each scroll through a curated feed reinforces the illusion that everyone else has it together—that their homes are pristine, their careers soaring, and their relationships picture-perfect. This constant comparison creates a toxic loop: the more we compare, the more inadequate we feel, and the more we push ourselves to measure up.

The effects of perfectionism aren't just emotional—they're physical too. Chronic stress, driven by the constant pursuit of perfection, wreaks havoc on the body. Elevated cortisol levels—our body's primary stress hormone—disrupt sleep, weaken the immune system, and increase the risk of cardiovascular disease. A study by Dr. Gordon Flett and colleagues found that perfectionism is linked to a range of physical health problems, from migraines to digestive issues. Over time, the strain of striving for an unreachable ideal can lead to burnout, a state of emotional, mental, and physical exhaustion. Burnout doesn't just rob you of productivity—it can steal your joy, your creativity, and even your sense of self.

Perfectionism also impacts relationships. When you hold yourself to impossible standards, you may project those expectations onto others. A partner who doesn't meet your ideals, a friend who doesn't reciprocate your level of effort, or a colleague who misses a deadline can become sources of frustration and disappointment. Research published in the *Journal of Personality and Social Psychology* reveals

that perfectionists often struggle with interpersonal conflicts, as their high expectations create tension and distance. Instead of fostering connection, perfectionism isolates.

Despite its costs, perfectionism persists because it promises something deeply appealing: control. If you can just
get everything right, it tells you, you can avoid the pain of
failure, criticism, or rejection. But this promise is a lie. Perfection is not only unattainable—it's unsustainable. No one
can live flawlessly, and the attempt to do so only tightens
the grip of fear and anxiety.

The irony of perfectionism is that it often undermines the
very goals it seeks to achieve. In the workplace, perfectionists may struggle with procrastination, unable to start a
project for fear it won't meet their standards. In creative
pursuits, they may stifle innovation, unwilling to take risks
that could lead to failure. In relationships, they may push
people away, unable to accept the imperfections that make
us human.

Breaking free from perfectionism begins with recognizing
its roots and challenging its assumptions. It means asking
yourself: What am I trying to prove? Who am I trying to impress? And what would happen if I let go of the need to be
perfect? These are not easy questions, but they are necessary ones. They open the door to a new way of thinking—
one that values progress over perfection, effort over outcome, and authenticity over appearance.

Perfectionism is not just a personal struggle; it's a societal
challenge. By rejecting the unrealistic standards imposed
by culture, media, and even our own minds, we create
space for something more meaningful: connection, growth,
and a life lived fully, rather than flawlessly.

Societal Pressures

From the moment we are old enough to comprehend the world around us, society begins to whisper in our ears: *Be better, achieve more, aim higher.* This whisper grows into a roar as we navigate life, shaping our beliefs about success, worth, and the standards we must meet. Society's obsession with control manifests in the ideals it sets—unrealistic, unforgiving, and omnipresent.

This cultural narrative is most apparent in what psychologists often describe as "hustle culture," a modern phenomenon where worth is equated with productivity. The mantra is everywhere: *You're only as valuable as the hours you work and the milestones you hit.* To rest is to be lazy, and to falter is to fail. Social media amplifies this ideology, serving as a 24/7 highlight reel of others' achievements. With every scroll, we're bombarded with images of carefully curated lives: the entrepreneur celebrating a million-dollar deal, the influencer jetting off to another exotic destination, the fitness guru posting yet another perfect workout routine.

What these images don't show is the truth behind the scenes: the exhaustion, the doubts, the missed moments of connection. Instead, we internalize an impossible standard. Leon Festinger's *Social Comparison Theory* highlights that humans naturally evaluate their worth by comparing themselves to others. However, the comparisons we make today are vastly different. Social media has turned them into an endless cycle, magnifying our awareness of what we *lack* rather than what we have. A 2020 study published in the *Journal of Social and Clinical Psychology* demonstrated that frequent social media use is directly correlated with heightened anxiety, depression, and dissatisfaction—consequences of unattainable comparisons.

Yet societal pressures extend beyond social media. They infiltrate our workplaces, relationships, and even our inner dialogues. In professional environments, the demand for control often materializes as perfectionism. Mistakes are not learning opportunities but marks of inadequacy. Deadlines are sacrosanct, even when meeting them comes at the expense of mental and physical health. This creates what organizational psychologists have termed "toxic productivity"—a culture where results are prioritized over well-being, leaving employees exhausted and unfulfilled. Research from the *Harvard Business Review* confirms that workplaces promoting perfectionism often experience higher turnover rates and decreased morale, as employees struggle to meet unreasonable expectations.

In relationships, the pressure to control is subtler but equally damaging. Many of us curate our personalities, presenting only the "acceptable" parts of ourselves to partners, friends, and family. Vulnerability becomes a risk, authenticity feels like a luxury, and the fear of judgment or rejection pushes us to maintain a facade. Over time, this performance erodes the trust and intimacy that genuine relationships require.

Perhaps the most insidious aspect of societal pressures is how seamlessly they blend into our daily lives. They don't announce themselves as harmful; instead, they masquerade as motivation. *Work harder,* they whisper. *Be better. Keep up.* And we listen—not because we lack awareness, but because we fear the consequences of falling behind.

Breaking free from these pressures requires us to confront the narratives we've absorbed—those invisible scripts that dictate how we measure success and worth. It means asking difficult questions: *Who benefits from my endless striving? What would happen if I redefined success for myself?* These questions may feel daunting, but they are the first step toward reclaiming control—not over life's outcomes, but over the way we choose to live.

Understanding how societal pressures intersect with perfectionism, fear, and anxiety reveals the full extent of their
grip on our lives. Together, these forces form a web that
feels impossible to escape. But escape is not only possible—it's essential for living authentically.

The Hidden Costs of Control

Control promises security, but its costs are often hidden
beneath the surface. The emotional toll of trying to control
every aspect of our lives can manifest as chronic stress,
strained relationships, and a diminished sense of self-
worth. Research shows that people who attempt to micromanage their environments are more likely to experience
anxiety and burnout, as their efforts to control often conflict
with the unpredictable nature of life.

Elijah's story is a powerful example. A young talented photographer and singer, Elijah built his life around his craft.
When the January 2025 California wildfires swept through
the Pacific Palisades, Elijah lost everything—his home, his
studio, and his equipment. "Watching it burn from the
street, powerless, was like watching my life unravel," he
said. Despite escaping unharmed, Elijah couldn't escape
the profound sense of loss. "I keep replaying it, wondering
what I could've done differently. But in the end, what could
I have controlled?"

Elijah's frustration highlights the trap many of us fall into:
believing that control can shield us from life's unpredictability. But when our control is shattered—whether by a natural disaster, a financial crisis, or a personal loss—the emotional weight can be devastating. Studies in psychology reveal that excessive need for control is linked to increased
feelings of helplessness and lower overall well-being.

I've faced this trap myself. When life spiraled out of control, I clung even tighter to the belief that I could manage my way through it. But each failed attempt to regain control only deepened my stress and eroded my confidence. It was only when I began to let go that I found a path forward—not by controlling the chaos, but by learning to adapt within it.

The truth is, life's greatest challenges often lie outside our control. The key is not to resist this truth but to embrace it. When we stop fighting against the currents, we free ourselves to focus on what we can influence: our mindset, our actions, and our capacity to grow.

At first glance, control appears to be the ultimate solution to life's unpredictability. It promises security, stability, and the satisfaction of achieving what we desire. Yet beneath its seemingly protective veneer lies a deeper truth: the more we cling to control, the more we compromise our well-being, creativity, and relationships. What we often fail to recognize is that control doesn't just fail to deliver on its promises—it exacts a heavy toll.

One of the most significant costs of control is its impact on mental health. When we obsessively try to manage every detail of our lives, we subject ourselves to chronic stress and anxiety. Studies published in the *Journal of Psychosomatic Research* show that individuals with high control-seeking tendencies experience elevated levels of cortisol, the body's primary stress hormone. While cortisol is crucial for managing short-term stress, prolonged exposure to elevated levels disrupts the body's natural rhythms, impairing immune function, disrupting sleep, and even increasing the risk of chronic illnesses like hypertension and diabetes.

This stress isn't limited to physical effects—it also takes a profound emotional toll. The constant effort to maintain control can lead to burnout, a state of emotional, physical, and mental exhaustion caused by prolonged stress. According to a 2019 report by the World Health Organization, burnout has become a global phenomenon, particularly in high-pressure environments where control and perfectionism are prioritized over balance and self-care. People who experience burnout often report feelings of cynicism, detachment, and a diminished sense of accomplishment, leaving them unable to enjoy even the successes they've worked so hard to achieve.

Control also narrows our perspective, limiting our ability to adapt and grow. In creative endeavors, for instance, the need to control every outcome can stifle innovation. Research from the *Creativity Research Journal* indicates that individuals who fear failure are less likely to take risks, experiment with new ideas, or explore unconventional solutions. This fear-driven approach inhibits not only creativity but also problem-solving—a crucial skill in navigating life's inevitable challenges.

Perhaps the most painful cost of control is the strain it places on relationships. When we attempt to manage others—whether through micromanagement, excessive expectations, or a refusal to delegate—we erode trust and create distance. A study in the *Journal of Social and Personal Relationships* found that individuals with high control needs often struggle to maintain close connections, as their behavior fosters resentment and inhibits genuine intimacy. Partners may feel stifled, friends may feel judged, and colleagues may become disengaged, leaving the person seeking control isolated in their efforts.

Despite these costs, the allure of control persists because it offers the illusion of certainty in an uncertain world. It tells us that if we just work harder, plan better, or push ourselves further, we can avoid pain, failure, and disappointment. Yet this promise is a mirage. Control does not eliminate uncertainty—it magnifies it. The more tightly we grip, the more we feel the weight of the unpredictable, and the more vulnerable we become to its inevitable disruptions.

The hidden costs of control extend beyond the personal, affecting the broader systems we inhabit. In workplaces, for example, a culture of excessive control can stifle collaboration, innovation, and morale. Teams operating under micromanagement often struggle with low productivity and high turnover, as employees feel undervalued and disengaged. In societal contexts, the pursuit of control manifests in policies and systems that prioritize order over equity, often exacerbating inequality and stifling progress.

Recognizing these hidden costs is the first step toward change. By understanding the toll control takes on our mental, emotional, and relational health, we can begin to question its role in our lives. What are we truly gaining—and losing—by holding on so tightly? This reflection is not about abandoning responsibility or effort; it's about redefining our approach to uncertainty and recognizing that sometimes, the greatest strength lies in letting go.

This shift in perspective prepares us to explore the transformative power of surrender—a concept that challenges our assumptions about control and reveals new possibilities for living fully and authentically.

Control as a Coping Mechanism

For many of us, control becomes a way of coping with the chaos of life. It offers an illusion of stability in an unstable world, a way to shield ourselves from the fear of uncertainty. But this coping mechanism often stems from deeper, unresolved fears—of failure, of vulnerability, of losing what we value most. Research suggests that people who rely on control to manage their emotions are more likely to experience heightened stress when faced with unpredictable situations.

I first learned to use control as a coping mechanism in childhood. My father's relentless expectations taught me that success was the only acceptable outcome and that failure was a sign of weakness. At the age of 13, the rule was that I was only allowed to sleep out if it was at my grandparents'. The only exception was a second cousin once removed who was my age and with whom I had grown a friendship since before I could remember. There was a condition however: I had to be back home first thing in the morning to catch up on my chores. I vividly recall one particular day, after staying overnight at the cousin-friend's house, I came back home in the afternoon, and on the three miles walk between the highway and the house, I didn't stop praying that my father would, by some miracle, have not noticed that I had broken the rule. By the time I reached our driveway and saw his car wasn't there, I felt both relieved and profoundly sorry for myself. That moment encapsulated my childhood: a constant juggling act to meet impossible expectations and avoid the consequences of failing to do so.

This pattern followed me into adulthood. During my third year of university, when I was failing academically, I clung to control as a lifeline. Instead of accepting the reality of my suspension, I threw myself into desperate attempts to reverse the decision—reaching out to distant family members, contacting university officials, even seeking intervention from an elected official. None of it worked. Instead, I found myself exhausted, humiliated, and no closer to a solution. The emotional toll of these attempts left me questioning my self-worth and forced me to confront a hard truth: my need for control wasn't saving me—it was consuming me.

Studies in behavioral psychology confirm that control, when used as a coping mechanism, often creates more harm than good. In one study, researchers found that individuals who overestimate their ability to influence outcomes are more likely to experience emotional burnout and interpersonal conflicts. What we often fail to see is that control isn't a shield against uncertainty—it's a weight that keeps us tethered to fear.

The good news is that by recognizing this pattern, we can begin to let go. Control might feel like a safety net, but it's often a trap. Learning to release it doesn't mean giving up—it means choosing freedom over fear.

The lessons learned from my early experiences weren't immediate. At first, I felt ashamed and defeated, but eventually, I began to see that my efforts to control everything were rooted in fear—fear of failure, fear of judgment, fear of being vulnerable. It's a fear many of us carry, often without realizing how much it drives our actions. The painful truth is that the need for control often stems from fear and insecurity, and its costs can be immense.

For many people, the need for control is not simply a preference or a personality trait—it is a response to something deeper. When life feels unpredictable, chaotic, or overwhelming, control becomes a way to create order. It provides a sense of safety in an uncertain world, a sense of power in the face of powerlessness. But like any coping mechanism, its effectiveness is limited, and its costs are often hidden.

The roots of control as a coping mechanism often lie in our past, particularly in experiences of trauma, loss, or instability. Childhood, in particular, plays a critical role. Research in developmental psychology has shown that children who grow up in unpredictable or chaotic environments— whether due to neglect, abuse, or frequent upheaval—are more likely to develop heightened control tendencies as adults. For these individuals, control becomes a way to compensate for the lack of stability they experienced early in life.

Take, for example, the case of a child growing up in a home where parental moods were unpredictable. One day, a parent might be loving and supportive; the next, angry and distant. In such an environment, the child may learn that their safety and sense of security depend on anticipating and managing the parent's emotional states. This might involve being overly compliant, striving for perfection, or suppressing their own needs to avoid conflict. Over time, these behaviors become internalized, setting the stage for a lifelong pattern of control.

Trauma survivors often experience a similar dynamic. A study published in the *Journal of Traumatic Stress* found that individuals who have endured significant trauma—such as a car accident, assault, or natural disaster—often develop a heightened need for control as a way to manage the unpredictability of life. For these individuals, control offers a psychological buffer against the feelings of helplessness and vulnerability that trauma often leaves behind. It becomes a way to reclaim agency, even if only temporarily.

However, while control may provide short-term relief, it rarely offers long-term healing. Instead, it can trap individuals in cycles of hypervigilance and overcompensation. The person who grew up walking on eggshells around an unpredictable parent may struggle to form healthy relationships as an adult, constantly trying to manage their partner's moods or actions. Similarly, the trauma survivor may find themselves obsessively planning every detail of their life, unable to tolerate even minor uncertainties. In both cases, the drive for control, though understandable, becomes a barrier to growth and connection.

The paradox of control as a coping mechanism is that it often reinforces the very feelings it seeks to alleviate. When we try to control every aspect of our lives, we inevitably encounter situations that are beyond our control. This failure to manage the unmanageable can trigger feelings of frustration, inadequacy, and even shame—emotions that further fuel the need for control. It's a self-perpetuating cycle that leaves little room for joy, spontaneity, or authentic connection.

Breaking free from this cycle begins with awareness. It requires us to recognize control not as a strength but as a response to pain—a way of coping with the uncertainty and unpredictability of life. This doesn't mean dismissing control as inherently bad; rather, it means examining when and why we reach for it. Are we trying to manage a difficult situation, or are we reacting to a deeper fear? Are we using control to navigate life's challenges, or are we using it to avoid them?

Healing also involves finding healthier ways to cope with uncertainty. Practices like mindfulness, which emphasize staying present and accepting the moment as it is, can be transformative. Studies published in the *Journal of Clinical Psychology* have shown that mindfulness-based interventions can reduce the need for control by helping individuals develop greater tolerance for ambiguity and discomfort. Therapy, too, can provide a safe space to explore the roots of control and develop new strategies for managing life's uncertainties.

Control may have served a purpose in the past, but it doesn't have to define the future. By understanding its origins and limits, we can begin to loosen its grip and make room for a life that is not just managed but truly lived. This understanding lays the foundation for exploring an even deeper truth: the illusion of control itself.

The Illusion of Control

At the heart of our need to control lies a fundamental misunderstanding: the belief that we have more power over life's outcomes than we actually do. Psychologists call this the *illusion of control*, a cognitive bias that leads us to overestimate our ability to influence events, even in situations governed largely by chance. This phenomenon is both comforting and deceptive, offering a sense of security while subtly setting us up for disappointment.

The illusion of control is deeply ingrained in human psychology. It stems, in part, from our desire to find patterns and make sense of the world. From an evolutionary perspective, recognizing patterns was essential for survival—understanding that rustling in the bushes might signal danger, for instance, helped our ancestors stay alive. However, this tendency to seek patterns can also lead us to perceive connections where none exist. Studies published in the *Journal of Personality and Social Psychology* show that people often attribute outcomes to their actions, even when those outcomes are determined by chance. A classic example is gambling, where players frequently believe their actions—how they roll the dice or how they select a lottery number—can influence the outcome, despite the randomness of the game.

This bias extends far beyond games of chance. In everyday life, we often overestimate our influence over events that are shaped by external factors. A manager might believe that their team's success hinges entirely on their leadership style, ignoring economic trends or market dynamics. A parent might attribute their child's behavior solely to their parenting methods, overlooking the child's temperament or peer influences. These beliefs, while comforting, create unrealistic expectations and set the stage for frustration when reality doesn't align with our efforts.

The illusion of control is particularly pronounced in high-stakes situations, where the consequences of uncertainty feel overwhelming. A patient facing a serious illness, for example, might meticulously follow every dietary recommendation and alternative therapy in the hope of controlling the disease's progression. While these efforts can provide a sense of agency and purpose, they can also lead to feelings of guilt or failure if the desired outcome isn't achieved. Research in the field of health psychology has shown that patients who overestimate their control in such scenarios are more likely to experience emotional distress, particularly when outcomes don't align with their expectations.

This phenomenon isn't confined to individuals—it permeates entire societies. Western culture, in particular, places a high value on personal agency and self-determination, promoting the idea that success is a direct result of effort and perseverance. While this mindset can be empowering, it also creates an environment where failure is viewed as a personal shortcoming rather than a natural part of life. The result is a culture that glorifies control and stigmatizes surrender, leaving little room for acceptance or resilience in the face of uncertainty.

The costs of the illusion of control are far-reaching. On an individual level, it can lead to anxiety, as we try to manage every detail of our lives in pursuit of outcomes we can't guarantee. It can also fuel perfectionism, as we convince ourselves that the key to success lies in flawless execution. In relationships, the illusion of control often manifests as micromanagement or overprotection, creating tension and eroding trust. On a societal level, this bias contributes to systemic problems, from the overreach of policies designed to eliminate every risk to the collective reluctance to embrace uncertainty as a natural part of life.

Breaking free from the illusion of control requires a fundamental shift in perspective. It begins with acknowledging the limits of our influence and recognizing that uncertainty is not a threat but a reality of existence. Practices like mindfulness and meditation can help cultivate this awareness, teaching us to accept the present moment without clinging to the need for control. As Jon Kabat-Zinn, a pioneer in mindfulness-based stress reduction, writes, "You can't stop the waves, but you can learn to surf."

Recognizing the illusion of control doesn't mean giving up or becoming passive. Rather, it means redirecting our energy toward what we can influence—our attitudes, decisions, and the effort we put into meaningful pursuits. By letting go of the need to control outcomes, we create space for growth, connection, and resilience. This perspective sets the stage for exploring the transformative power of surrender, which will be the focus of the next chapter.

Chapter 2: The Power of Surrender

Control feels safe. It promises us stability, order, and the power to shape our lives according to our desires. But as we've seen, that promise is often an illusion. Control comes at a cost—stress, isolation, and a relentless cycle of frustration when life refuses to conform to our plans. So, if control fails us, what's the alternative?

The answer lies in surrender. At first glance, surrender might seem like defeat, a passive acceptance of circumstances we can't change. But true surrender is far from weakness. It is an active, courageous choice to release the illusion of control and embrace life as it unfolds. Surrender doesn't mean giving up—it means letting go of the need to dictate every outcome and learning to navigate uncertainty with grace and resilience.

Surrender is a concept that challenges the very foundation of modern life. We live in a culture that glorifies control, equating it with strength, competence, and success. To surrender feels counterintuitive, even risky. Yet, history, psychology, and spirituality all point to the transformative power of letting go. When we stop clinging to what we cannot change, we free ourselves to focus on what we can: our mindset, our actions, and our capacity to grow.

This chapter explores what it truly means to surrender and why it's one of the most powerful tools we have for living a fulfilled life. You'll discover how letting go rewires your brain for creativity and resilience, why it reduces stress and fosters inner peace, and how it unlocks doors to possibilities you may never have imagined. Through science, stories, and reflection, you'll see that surrender isn't just an escape from the burdens of control—it's the key to living with authenticity, adaptability, and joy.

Let's begin by redefining surrender itself—starting with what it is, what it isn't, and why it has the potential to transform your life.

What Surrender Really Means

Surrender is a concept that is often misunderstood. For many, the word conjures images of defeat—a white flag raised in hopelessness, an acknowledgment of failure. It feels passive, even weak, in a culture that prizes determination and control. Yet true surrender is not about giving up; it's about letting go. It's an act of courage, a choice to release our attachment to outcomes we can't control and embrace the flow of life with openness and trust.

At its core, surrender is about perspective. It means shifting from a mindset of resistance to one of acceptance. Resistance says, *This isn't how things are supposed to be!* Acceptance says, *This is what is happening now—how will I respond?* This shift doesn't mean abandoning effort or resigning to circumstances; it means approaching life with flexibility, humility, and a willingness to adapt.

Surrender is deeply rooted in spiritual traditions across cultures. In Buddhism, the concept of *letting go* is central to the path of enlightenment. The Buddha taught that clinging—whether to desires, beliefs, or the illusion of control—leads to suffering. Similarly, Stoic philosophy emphasizes the importance of accepting what is beyond our control while focusing on what we can influence: our actions, choices, and character. As the Stoic philosopher Epictetus wrote, "Make the best use of what is in your power, and take the rest as it happens."

Modern psychology also supports the transformative power of surrender. Research in mindfulness and acceptance-based therapies has shown that letting go of rigid expectations reduces stress, enhances emotional well-being, and fosters greater resilience. A 2018 study published in the *Journal of Clinical Psychology* found that individuals who practiced mindfulness-based acceptance were better able to manage anxiety and respond constructively to life's challenges. By surrendering their need for certainty, these individuals developed a deeper sense of peace and clarity.

But what does surrender look like in practice? It's the athlete who learns to trust their training rather than obsess over the outcome of the race. It's the parent who releases their grip on their teenager's choices, allowing them to learn from their mistakes. It's the entrepreneur who accepts that failure is part of innovation, using setbacks as stepping stones rather than roadblocks. Surrender doesn't mean giving up effort—it means releasing the fear of failure and the need for total control.

Surrender is also an act of self-compassion. It acknowledges that we are human, that we cannot do everything or be everything. It frees us from the relentless pressure to be perfect, allowing us to approach life with kindness and curiosity rather than judgment. As Brené Brown, a researcher on vulnerability and shame, writes, "Perfectionism is not the same thing as striving to be your best. It's a shield. It's a way of thinking that says, 'If I look perfect, live perfect, and work perfect, I can avoid or minimize shame, blame, and judgment.'" Surrender breaks through this shield, inviting us to embrace our imperfections as part of our humanity.

One of the most profound aspects of surrender is its paradoxical nature: by letting go, we gain. We gain clarity, because we are no longer clouded by anxiety over outcomes. We gain freedom, because we release ourselves from the chains of perfectionism and control. And we gain strength, because surrender requires the courage to face uncertainty with an open heart and a steady mind.

This redefinition of surrender challenges the cultural narrative that equates control with strength and surrender with weakness. It asks us to see surrender not as a retreat but as an embrace of life's natural rhythm—a way of living that aligns us with the present moment rather than pulling us into the past or the future. Surrender is not the absence of action; it is action guided by wisdom, trust, and a deep understanding of what truly matters.

As we continue this chapter, we will explore the psychological benefits of letting go and how surrender can transform not only our inner world but also our relationships, creativity, and resilience. Letting go is not the end of the journey—it's the beginning of a new way of being.

The Psychological Benefits of Letting Go

Consider the practice of mindfulness. By focusing on the present moment, we let go of the need to control the future or dwell on the past. Research shows that mindfulness reduces stress, improves resilience, and enhances creativity by activating the brain's default mode network—a system that fosters problem-solving and emotional balance. Start with a simple exercise: spend five minutes observing your breath, allowing thoughts to come and go without judgment.

Letting go is more than a mindset; it's a transformative process that can profoundly impact our mental, emotional, and even physical well-being. When we relinquish the need to control every detail of our lives, we create space for resilience, creativity, and peace to flourish. These benefits are not just theoretical—they are deeply rooted in scientific research and real-world experiences.

One of the most immediate and noticeable benefits of letting go is the reduction of stress. When we try to micromanage every aspect of our lives, we place an enormous burden on ourselves. The body responds to this pressure by releasing stress hormones like cortisol, which, over time, can lead to a host of health problems, including anxiety, high blood pressure, and weakened immunity. Research published in *Psychosomatic Medicine* shows that individuals who practice mindfulness-based letting go experience significant reductions in stress and improved emotional regulation. Letting go interrupts the cycle of rumination—the repetitive, often negative thought patterns that fuel anxiety—allowing the mind to rest and reset.

Letting go also fosters emotional resilience. Resilience is not the absence of adversity but the ability to navigate it with grace and adaptability. When we stop clinging to the illusion of control, we become more open to life's uncertainties and better equipped to handle its challenges. Studies in positive psychology have found that individuals who cultivate an attitude of acceptance are more likely to recover quickly from setbacks, as they are less focused on resisting what they cannot change and more focused on finding solutions. This shift in perspective transforms obstacles into opportunities for growth.

Creativity is another area where the benefits of letting go are profound. The act of surrender allows us to step out of the rigid confines of perfectionism and into a state of flow—a mental state where we are fully immersed in the task at hand, free from self-doubt or fear of failure. Neuroscientific studies have shown that during flow states, the brain's prefrontal cortex—responsible for self-criticism and overthinking—temporarily quiets down, allowing for greater innovation and insight. Artists, writers, and entrepreneurs often describe their most inspired moments as those when they stopped trying to force ideas and instead allowed them to emerge naturally.

The psychological benefits of letting go extend beyond the individual to our relationships. Clinging to control often creates tension and conflict, as we impose our expectations on others or try to manage their behavior. Letting go, on the other hand, fosters trust and connection. It allows us to meet people where they are, to listen without judgment, and to embrace the imperfections that make relationships authentic and meaningful. A study published in the *Journal of Marriage and Family Therapy* found that couples who practiced acceptance and relinquished control over their partners' actions reported higher levels of satisfaction and intimacy.

Perhaps most profoundly, letting go brings a sense of inner peace. When we release the need to control outcomes, we free ourselves from the endless cycle of worry and striving. This doesn't mean we stop caring or working toward our goals; rather, it means we focus on what we can influence—our actions, attitudes, and responses—while letting go of the rest. As the poet Rumi beautifully expressed, "Try not to resist the changes that come your way. Instead, let life live through you. And do not worry that your life is turning upside down. How do you know that the side you are used to is better than the one to come?"

The benefits of letting go are not instant or automatic; they require practice and patience. But as we cultivate this skill, we begin to experience a life that is not only less stressful but also more creative, connected, and fulfilling. Letting go becomes a foundation for resilience and joy—a way of living that is deeply aligned with our true selves.

As we move forward in this chapter, we'll explore some of the common misconceptions about surrender and how to overcome them, paving the way for deeper understanding and transformation.

The Misconceptions About Surrender

Surrender is one of the most misunderstood concepts in our culture. At a glance, it's often equated with passivity, weakness, or even failure. For those raised in a world that glorifies grit and hustle, the idea of letting go can feel foreign, even threatening. Yet these misconceptions prevent us from embracing surrender as the powerful and transformative act that it truly is.

One of the most pervasive myths about surrender is that it means giving up. In a society that values relentless effort, the idea of letting go can feel like quitting. But surrender is not about abandoning your goals or resigning yourself to a life without action. Instead, it's about releasing the need to control outcomes you cannot guarantee. It's the recognition that while effort is within your power, results often are not. This shift in perspective allows you to channel your energy more effectively—toward the things you can influence rather than the things you can't.

Another common misconception is that surrender is a form of passivity. The truth is quite the opposite: surrender requires courage and strength. It takes bravery to acknowledge the limits of your control, to face uncertainty with openness, and to trust yourself to navigate life's challenges without clinging to rigid expectations. As psychologist Carl Rogers once wrote, "The curious paradox is that when I accept myself just as I am, then I can change." Surrender is not passive—it's the starting point for authentic growth and transformation.

The cultural narrative around surrender also often frames it as a loss of power. We are taught to believe that controlling everything is the ultimate sign of strength and competence. This belief is so deeply ingrained that surrender can feel like an admission of weakness or defeat. However, research in positive psychology challenges this notion. Studies published in *The Journal of Positive Psychology* have found that individuals who practice acceptance and letting go report higher levels of resilience and emotional well-being. By surrendering the illusion of control, they gain a deeper sense of personal power rooted in adaptability and self-trust.

Spiritual traditions, too, offer a counter-narrative to the cultural stigma around surrender. In Taoism, the principle of *wu wei*—often translated as "effortless action"—emphasizes harmony with the natural flow of life rather than forcing outcomes. Similarly, Christian teachings often highlight the power of surrendering to divine will, trusting that there is a greater plan beyond our immediate understanding. These philosophies remind us that surrender is not about inaction but about aligning our actions with a deeper wisdom and purpose.

Perhaps the most damaging misconception about surrender is that it makes us vulnerable to failure or exploitation. While it's true that letting go involves risk—it opens us to the possibility of loss—it also opens the door to connection, creativity, and growth. Vulnerability, as Brené Brown has famously argued, is not a weakness but a source of strength. It is through vulnerability that we form meaningful relationships, take bold steps toward our dreams, and experience life in its fullness.

Overcoming these misconceptions requires a shift in mindset. It means rethinking the stories we've been told about success, strength, and control. It means recognizing that surrender is not about relinquishing power but about redefining it. True power lies not in controlling everything but in knowing what to let go of and when. It's the power of presence, trust, and the willingness to adapt to life's ever-changing flow.

By reframing surrender as a strength rather than a weakness, we can begin to unlock its transformative potential. In the next section, we'll delve into real-world examples of surrender—stories of individuals who have let go and, in doing so, discovered resilience, freedom, and unexpected joy.

Stories of Transformation

Surrender is not a single act but a series of choices we make when life demands it. For me, one of those moments came during a meditation retreat—a turning point I could never have predicted. At the time, I had been months into studying the teachings of Kabbalah, desperately seeking answers to questions about my identity, my purpose, and my place in the world. I was carrying the weight of losses that felt too heavy to bear, trying to reconcile the shattered pieces of my life with the person I thought I was supposed to be.

The retreat was in the hills of Los Angeles, far from where I lived in Houston, Texas. I chose to drive the entire distance, believing that the solitude of the road might help me sort through the chaos in my mind. The journey itself felt symbolic—leaving behind the familiar in search of something greater. I arrived feeling skeptical, yet hopeful, uncertain of what I was about to encounter but willing to take the chance.

On arrival, after checking in, I decided to explore the forest behind the retreat cottage. It was a cool afternoon, and the sunlight filtered through the trees in a way that felt almost otherworldly. I wandered aimlessly, letting my feet guide me, until I came across a small clearing. The sunlight poured down in a perfect column, illuminating the space like a spotlight on a stage. And suddenly, I was no longer in the forest—I was back on the hill where I had grown up.

In that moment, everything came rushing back: the home I had left behind, the family I had tried so hard to please, the version of myself I had spent years trying to control. It felt as though the universe had led me full circle, bringing me face-to-face with the truths I had been avoiding. The weight of it all—the highs, the lows, the losses, the gains—hit me like a wave, and I fell to my knees.

I stayed there, kneeling in the light, as tears streamed down my face. It wasn't just sadness or regret—it was release. I realized, in that moment, that my life wasn't a series of mistakes or missed opportunities. It was a journey, perfectly imperfect, and every step had led me to that clearing in the forest. I wasn't in control of the grand design, but I was part of it. And that was enough.

For the first time in years, I felt an overwhelming sense of peace. Surrender wasn't about giving up—it was about trusting the process, about letting go of the need to control every outcome and allowing life to unfold as it was meant to. I sat in that clearing for what felt like hours, letting the light warm my face and the earth ground my body. When I finally stood up, I felt lighter, freer, as though I had left a part of myself behind in that forest—a part I no longer needed to carry.

That moment didn't fix everything. Life still demanded decisions, responsibilities, and resilience. But it shifted something fundamental within me. It taught me that surrender isn't a sign of weakness—it's an act of courage. It's the willingness to admit that we don't have all the answers and to trust that even in the uncertainty, there is purpose.

In my professional life, surrender became a tool for leadership. Filmmaking introduced me to artists who are as diverse in personality as they are united in their sensitivity. I learned that humility, empathy, and a willingness to share control created a collaborative environment. Actors, whether they were seasoned legends or rising stars, opened up to me not because I asserted authority but because I surrendered to the process, allowing space for mutual trust and respect. This approach not only made me a better filmmaker but also deepened my relationships.

These moments of surrender taught me that letting go isn't about giving up—it's about making space for growth, creativity, and connection.

Surrender is not a one-time act. It is a series of choices we make when life demands it. Sometimes, these choices arise from life-altering events, and other times they come from smaller, deeply personal realizations. Through the stories of others, we see how surrender reshapes the narrative of control, offering not defeat but renewal.

Los Angeles, January 2025: Destructive wildfires erupted simultaneously throughout Southern California, killing dozens, destroying more than 18 thousand homes and structures, and burning 57 thousand acres of land. In the weeks to follow, while volunteering at donation centers and YMCA centers, I met a few of my friends who lost everything they had in those fires.

Sally's story is not just one of loss but of reckoning with the fragility of control. A wife, mother, and leader in her community, Sally had built a life that felt solid, intentional, and secure. Her home in the Pacific Palisades was not only a sanctuary for her family but a symbol of everything she and her husband, Scott, had worked tirelessly to create. They had wealth, stability, and a sense of autonomy over their lives—until the fires came.

"When we came back, it was all ashes," Sally told me, her voice carrying a mix of disbelief and anger. "We worked so hard to build this life, to make sure our kids were safe, to have everything in place. And in one night, all of it was gone. We couldn't stop it, couldn't fix it. It just… happened. And that's the part that hurts the most."

For Sally, the financial loss wasn't the real devastation. What shook her to her core was the realization that no amount of planning, effort, or resources could have prevented what happened. "We've always been in control of everything—our careers, our home, our future. And now, for the first time, I feel like I don't even know what control means. How do you fight a fire? How do you stop something so big and uncontrollable?"

Her frustration grew as she tried to regain a sense of power. "I kept thinking, 'What can I do? How do I fix this?' But there was nothing—no plan, no solution, no way to undo what had been done. And that helplessness—it made me furious. I thought I was stronger than this, more prepared, but now I feel... small."

Sally's turning point came during a conversation with her husband. Scott, usually her partner in problem-solving, finally admitted his own sense of defeat. "He looked at me and said, 'I don't know how to fix this.' And that broke something in me—not in a bad way, but in a way that made me realize we were both trying to control the uncontrollable. It wasn't about fixing anymore. It was about accepting."

As Sally began to surrender to the reality of her situation, she found moments of clarity. "I realized that the fire didn't take everything. It didn't take my family, or our ability to move forward. And maybe we don't have control over everything we thought we did, but we do have control over how we respond."

Volunteering with other displaced families became her way of regaining a sense of agency. "It gave me purpose," she said. "I couldn't control what had happened to us, but I could control how I showed up for others. Helping them made me feel less powerless—it reminded me that even in the middle of chaos, we can find ways to make a difference."

Sally's journey wasn't about regaining the control she had lost—it was about redefining what control meant. "I've realized that life isn't something you can perfectly plan or protect. It's messy, unpredictable, and sometimes it's downright cruel. But in that messiness, there's still room for choice—for deciding who you want to be when the storm clears."

Her story is a powerful reminder that surrender isn't about giving up—it's about finding strength in the face of helplessness. Sally's surrender didn't erase her grief or frustration, but it allowed her to channel them into something meaningful. It's this kind of surrender—not to the fire, but to the reality of life's unpredictability—that ultimately sets us free.

Elijah's story is one of despair and rediscovery. At 34, he had built a life that revolved around his creativity. A renowned photographer and an up-and-coming singer, his identity was intertwined with his art. His home, perched in the Pacific Palisades, was more than just a place to live—it was a studio, a gallery, and a sanctuary. But when the wildfires swept through his neighborhood, everything was reduced to ashes.

"My house, my studio, my cameras—they weren't just things. They were part of me, part of who I am," Elijah told me. Elijah's frustration wasn't just about the material loss. It was about the helplessness he felt. He had spent years meticulously crafting a life where everything was under his control, and in one night, it was gone. "I've always been the guy with a plan, the one who knows what's next. But standing there, watching everything I'd built disappear, I felt like a kid again—scared, small, and powerless."

For weeks, Elijah struggled to find his footing. He replayed the events over and over, asking himself what he could have done differently. "Should I have moved my studio somewhere else? Should I have had a better evacuation plan? But no matter how many questions I asked, the answer was always the same: there was nothing I could've done. And that's what made it so hard to accept."

His turning point came when he stopped trying to rewrite the past and began to embrace the present. Without a studio or equipment, Elijah turned to his phone—a tool he had never considered worthy of his art. "At first, it felt ridiculous. I mean, what could I create with a phone? But then I started taking photos of the aftermath—the charred trees, the smoky skies, the way life still found a way to push through the ashes."

These photos, raw and unfiltered, carried a depth Elijah had never explored before. They told a story of loss, yes, but also of resilience. "Surrendering to the reality of my situation didn't take away my creativity—it gave me a new perspective. It showed me that my art wasn't in the tools I used but in the way I saw the world."

Elijah's story is a testament to the transformative power of letting go. By surrendering the illusion of control, he found freedom—not freedom from loss, but freedom to create and rebuild in ways he hadn't imagined. "I'm still figuring it out," he admitted, "but I know this: the fire didn't take everything. It gave me something too. A reminder that life is fragile, yes, but also resilient. And so am I."

Letting go matters because it's not just an act—it's a mindset, a shift in how we approach life's unpredictability. The stories of Sally and Elijah illustrate this truth in vivid detail. For Sally, surrender was about accepting that her family's strength didn't come from controlling every aspect of their lives but from facing challenges together. For Elijah, it was about rediscovering the essence of his creativity when everything he thought defined him was stripped away.

But why does letting go feel so unnatural? Neuroscience gives us part of the answer. Our brains are hardwired to seek control as a survival mechanism. When faced with uncertainty, the amygdala—the brain's fear center—triggers a stress response, urging us to act. This instinct, while protective in moments of immediate danger, often works against us in the complexities of modern life. Studies show that clinging to control in uncontrollable situations doesn't reduce stress; it amplifies it.

The societal messages we receive compound this struggle. We're told that success is the result of meticulous planning, unrelenting effort, and absolute control. Yet, as Sally and Elijah learned, no amount of planning can account for life's unpredictability. The wildfires didn't care about Sally's routines or Elijah's vision for his future—they came, and they took. The only choice left was how to respond.

Letting go doesn't mean giving up. It means acknowledging what we cannot change and choosing to focus on what we can. It means finding strength not in control but in adaptability, not in resistance but in resilience. This shift isn't easy, but it's transformative. Research shows that individuals who practice acceptance and surrender report greater emotional well-being and higher levels of creativity and problem-solving.

When we let go, we create space—for healing, for growth, for possibilities we couldn't see when we were blinded by the need to control. Sally found that space in her family's shared vulnerability, in showing her children that grief and resilience can coexist. Elijah found it in his art, in the freedom to create without the constraints of perfection. And we, too, can find it in our lives, if we're willing to let go of what we think we need and embrace what life offers instead.

Surrender isn't about losing—it's about opening. Opening to the lessons hidden in loss, the strength found in vulnerability, and the beauty that emerges when we stop fighting the current and start flowing with it. It is a concept that can feel abstract until we see it in action. Stories of real people who have embraced letting go reveal the profound and transformative power of surrender. These narratives show us that letting go is not about defeat—it's about finding strength, clarity, and growth in life's most challenging moments.

One powerful example of surrender comes from Nelson Mandela. During his 27 years of imprisonment, Mandela faced unimaginable hardship. He could have succumbed to anger and despair, clinging to the bitterness of being wrongfully imprisoned. Instead, he chose a path of surrender—not to his circumstances but to the higher purpose of his life. By letting go of his need for vengeance and control over immediate outcomes, Mandela found peace within himself and emerged as a leader who united a fractured nation. His surrender wasn't passive; it was an active choice to rise above his circumstances, to trust in the long arc of justice, and to focus on what he could influence: his mindset, his values, and his vision for the future.

Another inspiring story of surrender comes from Elizabeth Gilbert, the author of *Eat, Pray, Love*. After experiencing a painful divorce and a crisis of identity, Gilbert set out on a journey of self-discovery. Her travels through Italy, India, and Indonesia were less about escaping her problems and more about surrendering to the process of healing. In her book, Gilbert writes about the moment she realized that clinging to her pain was preventing her from finding peace. "I was not rescuing myself," she reflects, "by being miserable over my failed marriage. I was only hurting myself further." By letting go of her need to understand or fix everything, she opened herself to new experiences and, ultimately, a renewed sense of purpose and joy.

Surrender also plays a pivotal role in the world of innovation. Take the story of Thomas Edison. When his laboratory burned down in 1914, destroying years of research, Edison responded with an attitude of acceptance rather than despair. "There is great value in disaster," he famously said. "All our mistakes are burned up. Thank God we can start anew." Edison's ability to surrender to circumstances beyond his control allowed him to pivot, rebuild, and continue his groundbreaking work. His resilience reminds us that surrender isn't about giving up—it's about finding the courage to begin again.

On a more personal level, I experienced a profound moment of surrender myself during the financial collapse in

Lebanon. When the banking system fell apart, it didn't just wipe out my savings—it stripped away the foundation of stability I had spent years building. At first, I did everything in my power to regain control. There were sleepless nights, endless calculations, and desperate attempts to salvage what could be saved. But eventually, I had to face the truth: no amount of effort could change what had already been lost. Letting go wasn't easy—it never is. Yet it was in surrendering to the reality of the situation that I found a way forward. Instead of being defined by the loss, I focused on what I could control: my adaptability, resilience, and ability to rebuild. Piece by piece, I began to create a new foundation—not by resisting the change, but by embracing it.

What these stories have in common is not the absence of struggle but the presence of a profound shift in perspective. Surrender allowed Mandela to find freedom in the midst of captivity, Gilbert to rediscover her sense of self, Edison to innovate in the face of loss, and me to rebuild after financial upheaval. Each of us faced circumstances that were beyond our control, yet through surrender, we found resilience, creativity, and a deeper connection to our purpose.

These stories remind us that surrender is not a one-size-fits-all process. It looks different for everyone and unfolds in its own time. But what remains constant is its power to transform our relationship with ourselves, others, and the world around us. By letting go, we gain the freedom to live more authentically, to adapt to life's challenges with grace, and to open ourselves to possibilities we might never have imagined.

Surrender isn't about giving up—it's about creating space for growth. When we let go of the need to control everything, we open ourselves to new possibilities. Whether it's finding strength in vulnerability, creativity in chaos, or connection in shared struggles, surrender allows us to see life not as a series of obstacles but as an evolving journey. In the next chapter, we'll explore how to break the control habit and take the first steps toward a more liberated way of living.

Chapter 3: The Illusion of Control

The Seductive Power of Control

Control has a way of seducing us, whispering promises of certainty in an uncertain world. It convinces us that with enough effort, planning, and precision, we can shape life exactly as we want it. We cling to this belief, not because it's always true, but because it feels safer than facing the unpredictable. For me, this illusion came into sharp focus during a journey from Dubai to Mexico City—an experience that would shake my confidence in control to its core.

I was in a hurry to get back to Mexico City after a short stint in Dubai. There were no direct flights, but that didn't faze me. I saw the logistical challenges not as obstacles but as puzzles to solve. After hours of comparing flights, I booked two separate tickets: one from Dubai to Paris' Orly Airport and another from Charles de Gaulle (CDG) to Mexico City. The catch? The two airports were on opposite sides of Paris, and I had just two hours between landing at Orly and taking off from CDG.

This wasn't recklessness—it was confidence. I had accounted for everything: the punctuality of the flights, the efficiency of Parisian transport, and my own ability to navigate it all. The plan felt airtight, a testament to my ability to manage even the most complex scenarios.

But life, as always, had other plans.

The first flight landed on time, but instead of disembarking smoothly, we were directed to a tube under maintenance. Minutes ticked by as the crew struggled to find an alternative. When they finally opened the doors, we were ushered onto a bus—a mere 40 yards from the gate, yet it took another 45 minutes before we were allowed to leave. Inside the suffocating bus, watching the gate just steps away, I felt the first cracks in my confidence.

Once inside the terminal, chaos reigned. I raced through Orly Airport, my heart pounding as I navigated customs and passport control. By the time I stumbled outside, it was clear I wouldn't make it to CDG in time. Still clinging to the illusion of control, I jumped on the first train I could find—only to realize it was a slow local train. Frustration bubbled over. In my desperation to correct the mistake, I got off at an intermediate stop, hoping to catch the express. But the express train was delayed, and I stood on the platform, helpless and fuming, as precious minutes slipped away. Eventually, I called an Uber, paying a fortune to race to CDG. But by the time I arrived, the gate was closed.

Sitting in that airport, waiting for the next available flight—one that was delayed and eventually canceled—I had plenty of time to reflect. I had spent the better part of 24 hours running on adrenaline, believing that if I just tried hard enough, I could outmaneuver circumstances beyond my control. But my efforts had been futile. I wasn't in control of the maintenance delays, the customs lines, the train schedules, or even the weather. All my planning, all my confidence, had led me to this: stranded, exhausted, and painfully aware of my own limits.

This experience was a stark reminder of the illusion of control—the belief that we can influence outcomes far beyond our actual reach. Psychologists refer to this as a cognitive bias, one that gives us a false sense of certainty in a chaotic world. Studies show that this illusion is rooted in our brain's need to calm the fear response triggered by uncertainty. The promise of control is comforting, but it is rarely true. And when reality shatters that illusion, the emotional fallout can be devastating.

Sitting in the airport that night, I realized that control had seduced me not because I needed to manage the details of my journey, but because I was afraid of what would happen if I didn't. The illusion of control had given me a false sense of security, one that collapsed the moment life threw me off course. In the end, the truth was simple: I had never been in control. I had merely convinced myself I was, and the price of that delusion was frustration, exhaustion, and an airport floor for a bed.

Recognizing this illusion is the first step toward freedom. It doesn't mean abandoning effort or preparation—it means understanding that no matter how much we plan, life will always have the final say. Letting go of the need for control isn't about giving up—it's about finding the strength to adapt, to trust, and to move forward when life takes an un-expected turn.

How the Illusion of Control Manifests

If the illusion of control is the belief that we can bend life to our will, then its manifestations are the countless ways we attempt to tighten our grip on everything around us. It shows up in how we manage our work, our relationships, and even our daily habits, often without us realizing it. We plan, micromanage, and overanalyze, hoping that if we control every detail, we can prevent failure, avoid pain, or ensure success. But what we fail to see is that this very need for control often creates the tension, frustration, and conflicts we're trying to avoid.

I experienced this firsthand during the development of my Film Society app. It was a project I had spent years dream-ing about, and finally, after months of preparation, I de-cided to bring it to life. Hiring my friend Arvind, who had re-cently started his own app development business, felt like the perfect choice. He was talented, motivated, and some-one I trusted deeply. I was certain that with him leading the development team, the project would be a success.

At first, everything seemed to be on track. The team was productive, communication was smooth, and I felt confident in my decision. But as the deadline approached, progress began to lag. My confidence turned to anxiety. The app wasn't just another project—it was a reflection of years of ambition and effort. The thought of missing the deadline felt like failure, and I couldn't bear the idea of losing control.

Instead of discussing my concerns openly with Arvind, I took matters into my own hands. I inserted myself into the team's weekly meetings, convinced that my involvement would speed things up. I thought my input would provide clarity, solve problems, and create urgency. What I didn't realize was that my presence was doing the opposite.

The team, accustomed to their own workflow and language, suddenly found themselves navigating my feedback—feedback that often disrupted their priorities. I misunderstood technical details, misjudged timelines, and inadvertently shifted their focus away from what truly mattered. My micromanagement created tension, confusion, and delays, and the atmosphere became strained. What I saw as helpful guidance, they saw as interference. By the time the deadline came and went, the project was not only behind schedule but also burdened by the tension I had introduced.

Reflecting on this experience, I realized that my need for control wasn't about the app itself—it was about me. The app represented years of dreaming, planning, and hoping, and the fear of failure had triggered my need to micromanage. It was as if by exerting control over the team, I was trying to convince myself that I still had control over the outcome. But in doing so, I had undermined the very collaboration and trust that were essential to the project's success.

This is how the illusion of control manifests: we cling to the details, believing that if we can manage every piece, we can guarantee the whole. But life rarely works that way. Control is seductive because it offers the illusion of certainty, but when it fails, it leaves us with more than just disappointment—it leaves us disconnected from the people and processes that truly matter.

Psychologists describe this tendency as an overestimation of influence—a cognitive bias that convinces us we have power where we do not. Research shows that this bias is particularly strong in high-pressure situations, where fear of failure amplifies our desire to control. But as I learned through the Film Society project, this illusion often backfires. The harder we cling, the more we lose sight of what's important: trust, collaboration, and the ability to adapt.

Letting go of the illusion of control isn't easy, especially in a world that glorifies self-reliance and perfectionism. But it's necessary. The more we loosen our grip, the more space we create for innovation, connection, and growth. As I learned the hard way, control isn't the solution—it's often the problem. And only by recognizing this can we begin to find a better way forward.

The Costs of Clinging to Control

The costs of clinging to control are not always obvious. They creep in like a slow tide, eroding our emotional reserves, straining our relationships, and leaving our bodies to bear the burden. The more we try to manage everything, the more we lose—time, energy, connection, and even health. Yet we persist, convinced that holding on is the only way to move forward.

Clinging to control creates an endless loop of tension and burnout. When we insist on managing every detail, we tie our sense of worth to outcomes that are often beyond our influence. For me, this became painfully clear during the most intense period of my filmmaking career. Over the course of a year and a half, I juggled multiple productions across three continents, living out of a suitcase with barely enough time to catch my breath.

On paper, it looked like a life many would envy—jet-setting between North America, Europe, and the Middle East, working on exciting creative projects. But beneath the surface, it was a relentless grind. I drove myself harder with each passing day, convinced that I needed to stay on top of every decision, every meeting, every detail. Rest felt like a luxury I couldn't afford.

At first, the adrenaline masked the toll it was taking. But as the months wore on, I found myself increasingly irritable, anxious, and disconnected from the joy of the work I loved. Nights became sleepless as my mind raced with what-ifs and to-do lists. The harder I pushed, the more I felt the weight of everything I was trying to control. Burnout wasn't a sudden collapse—it was a slow unraveling, a loss of energy and purpose that left me questioning not just my work but my identity.

Psychologists have long studied the emotional toll of control. Research shows that individuals with high control tendencies often experience greater levels of stress and anxiety, particularly in unpredictable situations. The need to control isn't just exhausting—it's self-perpetuating, as each failure to manage the uncontrollable deepens our determination to try harder.

Control doesn't just take a toll on us—it affects the people around us. When we micromanage or impose our expectations on others, we create tension and distance. During my most intense work period, I began to notice these effects in my relationships. Friends who admired my determination grew frustrated by my rigidity. Collaborators who once enjoyed working with me felt the strain of my perfectionism.

One project in particular stands out. It was a collaborative effort involving several talented artists, and I took it upon myself to oversee every aspect of the production. My intentions were good—I wanted the project to be a success—but my need for control led to friction. Instead of fostering trust and creativity, I stifled it. My collaborators began to pull back, and the project, which had started with so much promise, became a source of tension.

The hardest lesson I've learned is that relationships thrive not on control but on trust. When we try to control others, we undermine the very connection we seek. We send the message that their efforts aren't enough, that their ideas don't matter. Over time, this erodes not just the relationship but the mutual respect that sustains it.

Our bodies, too, bear the weight of control. During that same period, I developed a severe rotator cuff injury in my left shoulder. It was the result of hauling heavy suitcases up staircases, along streets, and through airports without rest. I ignored the pain, convincing myself that I could push through it. After all, I had more pressing things to worry about—meetings to attend, deadlines to meet, projects to oversee.

But the pain grew worse, until it became impossible to ignore. A doctor later told me that my lifestyle—my relentless drive to keep going—was responsible for the injury. His words were a wake-up call: "Your body is telling you to stop," he said. "If you don't listen, the consequences will be far worse."

In that moment, I realized how much I had sacrificed in the name of control. The headaches, the insomnia, the chronic tension in my shoulders and back—they weren't just symptoms of a busy life. They were my body's way of screaming for relief.

This isn't uncommon. Chronic stress, often fueled by the need for control, has been linked to a host of physical ailments, from migraines to heart disease. The body, as trauma expert Dr. Bessel van der Kolk puts it, "keeps the score." And when we refuse to listen, the price can be devastating.

The costs of clinging to control are undeniable, but they are not inevitable. Recognizing them is the first step toward freedom. It's not about giving up or resigning ourselves to chaos—it's about finding a new way forward. It's about learning to trust ourselves, our relationships, and the process of life, even when things don't go as planned.

In the end, letting go isn't about losing—it's about reclaiming. Reclaiming our energy, our connections, and our wellbeing. And while it's not an easy journey, it's one worth taking.

Recognizing the Illusion

To move beyond the illusion of control, we must first learn to recognize it for what it is—a fragile mirage. It feels solid, comforting, even empowering, until life's winds sweep through and leave us grasping at emptiness. For so long, I believed that control was my strength, my armor against chaos. It wasn't until life forced me to confront the limits of my influence that I began to see the truth: control wasn't protecting me—it was holding me back.

One of the most sobering moments in my journey came during a layover in Beirut, on my way from Dubai to New York. I was on autopilot, moving from one responsibility to the next without pause. My shoulder pain—persistent, gnawing, and worsening—had become impossible to ignore. Reluctantly, I stopped at a clinic and underwent some tests. The doctor's voice on the phone was calm but firm: "You need surgery and a year of rehabilitation. This isn't something you can push through."

I remember sitting in the departure lounge, his words echoing in my mind. For years, I had built my life around the belief that I could will my way through anything. I ignored pain, dismissed exhaustion, and saw every obstacle as a problem to solve. But this wasn't something I could outwork or outthink. My body had drawn a line, one that no amount of determination could cross. In that moment, I felt stripped bare—not just of control, but of the illusion that I had ever truly possessed it.

Recognizing the illusion of control isn't always as dramatic as a wake-up call from a doctor. More often, it's the subtle, persistent signs that we overlook in our daily lives. It's the way we overthink decisions, endlessly replaying scenarios in our minds, convinced that one wrong move will ruin everything. It's the anxiety that bubbles up when plans fall apart, leaving us feeling untethered and vulnerable. It's the strain in our relationships when we try to manage not just our own lives, but the emotions and actions of those around us.

These behaviors may feel like harmless quirks, but they come at a cost. Overthinking leads to paralysis, preventing us from moving forward. Anxiety erodes our peace of mind, making us reactive instead of intentional. And controlling others creates tension and mistrust, driving wedges into our most important connections.

Psychologists describe this as an overestimation of control—a cognitive bias that gives us a false sense of influence over our environment. While this bias can provide short-term comfort, it ultimately sets us up for disappointment when reality doesn't conform to our expectations. The harder we cling to control, the more we amplify our own suffering.

For many, the moment of recognition comes not by choice but by necessity. It happens when life strips us of the illusion, forcing us to confront what we've been avoiding. A failed relationship, a missed opportunity, an unexpected tragedy—these are the moments that reveal the limits of our control and challenge us to rethink how we navigate the world.

For me, this process wasn't a single moment but a series of realizations over time. It was in the nights spent reflecting on what truly mattered, in the meditations that quieted my mind enough to see clearly, and in the conversations with loved ones who reminded me that surrender isn't weakness—it's wisdom. Each small shift brought me closer to understanding that control wasn't the source of my strength. It was a barrier to it.

Recognizing the illusion of control isn't about giving up. It's about gaining perspective. It's about seeing life not as something to conquer, but as something to experience. It's about accepting that uncertainty is not the enemy—it's the canvas on which possibility is painted.

Letting go doesn't mean resigning yourself to chaos. It means choosing trust over fear, adaptability over rigidity, and connection over isolation. It means shifting your focus from what you can't control to what you can: your mindset, your actions, and your capacity to grow.

This shift isn't easy, but it's transformative. It frees us from the exhausting cycle of trying to control the uncontrollable. It allows us to embrace life as it is, not as we wish it to be. And in doing so, it opens the door to a kind of freedom we never thought possible.

In the next chapter, we'll explore what happens when we take that step—when we let go of the illusion and focus on what truly matters. Because while we can't control everything, we can control how we respond. And that makes all the difference.

Chapter 4: The Freedom of Letting Go

The Paradox of Freedom

At first, the idea of letting go feels counterintuitive. We're taught to hold on—to our ambitions, our relationships, our plans—because to let go is to lose. Society reinforces this constantly: push harder, fight for control, never back down. To surrender, we're told, is to admit defeat.

Yet, paradoxically, the opposite is often true. The tighter we cling, the more exhausted we become. The more we fight to control the uncontrollable, the more powerless we feel. But when we release our grip, when we trust in something greater than ourselves, a new kind of freedom emerges—not the absence of effort, but the presence of peace.

I rarely thought of quitting as a path to freedom. If anything, I feared it. I saw it as failure, as a betrayal of persistence and effort. I was someone who tried to fix things before they even broke. I believed that with enough willpower, I could make anything work.

And yet, I always felt a deep, unspoken relief when a troubled relationship ended. The weight I carried would disappear, and the air would feel lighter, even if pain still lingered.

Joe was the perfect example. From the moment we met, he saw something in me—something I hadn't yet learned to see in myself. His certainty convinced me of an "us" before I even had time to wonder if it was what I wanted. We moved in together, and for a time, it worked. We were compatible in many ways, but something shifted. It became about him. My desires, my dreams, and even my identity began to recede into the background, and yet I clung on. I convinced myself that if I just tried harder, if I gave more, I could preserve what we had.

Even when it became humiliating, even when it became psychopathic, I stayed. I held on, hoping to force what was clearly slipping away. I wasn't waiting for happiness—I was waiting for a sign, a moment of undeniable truth that would tell me it was time to walk away. But that moment never came. Instead, Joe ended it.

And then, in the pain of abandonment, I felt something I didn't expect—relief. The very thing I had fought to preserve had become my prison, and now, I was free. I was free to be myself again. Free to breathe. Free to want things for myself.

That moment was one of the first times I truly understood the paradox of letting go. I had clung so tightly, believing I was protecting something precious, but in reality, I was suffocating. And when I finally loosened my grip—when I was forced to—I discovered something I never expected: freedom.

The truth is, surrender doesn't mean giving up. It means making space. It means trusting that there is something beyond what we can see, that our grip on life doesn't define its course. When we let go, we don't fall—we fly.

The Science Behind Letting Go

If letting go feels unnatural, that's because, biologically, it is. Our brains are wired for control.

The human mind craves certainty. From an evolutionary perspective, control meant survival. Early humans who could predict their environment—where to find food, how to avoid danger—had a distinct advantage. The desire to shape our surroundings and anticipate outcomes is deeply embedded in our neurobiology.

But what happens when we cling to control in a world that refuses to be controlled?

Studies in neuropsychology have shown that the brain's default mode network (DMN)—the part responsible for self-referential thinking—activates when we overanalyze, ruminate, or obsess over control. The more we try to grasp control, the more active this network becomes, fueling anxiety, stress, and overthinking.

Letting go, on the other hand, engages the prefrontal cortex, which regulates emotions and promotes adaptability. When we stop resisting uncertainty and accept life as it comes, our brains shift into a more relaxed, creative, and resilient state.

Functional MRI (fMRI) studies have demonstrated that practices like mindfulness and meditation—both rooted in the principle of surrender—reduce amygdala activity, the part of the brain responsible for fear and emotional reactivity. In other words, the more we practice letting go, the more we train our brains to experience peace instead of panic in the face of uncertainty.

Control provides a dopamine hit—the same neurotransmitter linked to pleasure and reward. Every time we micromanage a situation, predict an outcome, or successfully impose order, our brains reward us with a fleeting sense of relief.

But like any addiction, the effects are temporary. The moment uncertainty creeps in, we seek control again, repeating the cycle. This is why people who struggle with anxiety or perfectionism often describe an exhausting loop of overthinking—one that never truly brings peace.

Surrender breaks this cycle. When we accept what we cannot control, our brains stop fighting reality. Stress hormones like cortisol decrease, while serotonin levels rise, bringing an overall sense of well-being.

Dr. David Hawkins, in his work Letting Go: The Pathway of Surrender, describes how resistance is what creates suffering, not the circumstances themselves. When we resist reality—whether it's a loss, a failure, or an uncertain future—we create inner conflict.

Surrender, however, is a state of alignment with life rather than a battle against it. Psychological research has consistently shown that individuals who practice acceptance and flexibility report higher levels of life satisfaction, emotional stability, and resilience.

One study on radical acceptance found that people who embraced life's unpredictability, rather than fought against it, experienced lower stress levels, stronger emotional regulation, and even improved immune function.

Understanding the science behind letting go isn't just an abstract concept—it's a revolutionary shift in how we approach life.

When we stop fighting for control, our minds become clearer. We become more creative, more adaptable, and more at peace. Stress no longer dominates our decision-making, and fear no longer dictates our actions.

In the next section, we'll explore real-life stories of people—including myself—who discovered profound freedom the moment they finally let go.

Stories of Liberation

Letting go is not an abstract theory—it is a lived experience. For some, surrender arrives in a quiet moment of acceptance; for others, it is thrust upon them through loss, hardship, or the unraveling of a carefully constructed life.

I have lived both versions.

There are few moments in life when we are forced to confront how little control we truly have. For me, that moment came when I lost everything—my wealth, my business, my sense of identity. It was a stripping away so complete that I had no choice but to let go.

For the first time, I was not defined by what I had built, but by what remained after it was gone. And what remained was me—raw, unburdened, and free from the expectations I had spent decades upholding. It was terrifying at first. I had measured success by accomplishments, by ownership, by the validation of others. Now, stripped of it all, I had to redefine what success meant.

And I did. In surrendering to the unknown, I found something far greater than the illusion of control—I found peace. No longer tethered to outdated definitions of achievement, I began to live fully in the present. The weight I had carried for years—the need to prove myself, the fear of failing—was gone.

And in that emptiness, there was room to breathe, to grow, to be.

Sally had spent years crafting the perfect life. She and her husband, Scott, built a home in the Pacific Palisades, raised three children, and contributed meaningfully to their community. Their life was structured, planned, and secure—until the fires came.

In a single night, everything was gone.

The house they built, the carefully curated memories, the routines that had defined their days—it was all reduced to ash. At first, Sally's instinct was to fix the situation, to regain control, to piece life back together as it had been before. But nothing could undo what had happened. No amount of planning, saving, or strategizing could restore what was lost.

"I kept asking myself what I was supposed to do next," she told me. "But I think the real question was, who am I now?"

In the wake of destruction, Sally found a truth she had never faced before: her sense of control had always been an illusion. She had believed that her choices, her discipline, and her meticulous planning had made her life what it was. But in reality, she had never been in control.

For weeks, she fought against grief, clinging to what had been. But eventually, she surrendered—not to despair, but to the flow of life itself. She realized that control had never been what held her family together. It was love, resilience, and presence.

"I thought we lost everything," she said. "But when I finally let go of what I thought life was supposed to be, I saw what was left. And what was left was my family, my strength, and the chance to rebuild—not just a house, but a deeper, more meaningful life."

Elijah had spent his life mastering his craft—both as a celebrity photographer and a singer. His home, his studio, his tools—everything that made his art possible—was built over years of hard work. And then, in a matter of hours, it was gone.

Standing in front of what used to be his home, Elijah felt the weight of loss crash over him. He had controlled everything—his career, his image, his trajectory. Now, none of it seemed to matter.

For days, he was lost in a fog of disbelief. The more he tried to hold on to what was, the more painful it became. "I kept replaying everything in my head," he told me. "Trying to figure out what I could have done differently, as if there was some way to rewrite the past."

Then came the moment of surrender.

"I realized I had a choice," he said. "I could let this loss define me, or I could let it free me."

And in that decision, everything shifted. Instead of seeing himself as a man who lost everything, he began to see himself as a man with nothing left to lose—and that was liberating.

For the first time in years, he wasn't bound by the expectations he had placed on himself. He didn't have to uphold a brand, maintain a status, or prove himself to anyone. He was free to create, to rebuild, to step into something new.

"Elijah before the fire was trying to control everything. Elijah after the fire? He's just here to live."

Sally and Elijah's stories, like my own, are proof that the freedom we seek doesn't come from control—it comes from surrender.

We spend our lives gripping so tightly onto what we think we need: the career, the relationship, the plan. But true freedom is found in releasing our grip and trusting that life will unfold exactly as it's meant to.

Surrender doesn't mean passivity—it means trust. It means knowing that even when the ground shifts beneath us, we are still standing. It means choosing presence over anxiety, flow over resistance, and faith over fear.

Because when we stop clinging to the illusion of control, we finally understand the truth:

We were never meant to force life. We were meant to live it.

Now that we've explored how letting go leads to liberation, the next step is redefining what success actually means when we stop measuring it by outdated metrics.

The Freedom to Redefine Success

For most of my life, success had a clear definition. It was tangible, measurable, and, in many ways, dictated by society. Success meant achievement, wealth, recognition, and proof of my worth. It meant constantly striving for the next milestone, the next project, the next validation.

But when life stripped me of everything—the wealth, the career, the identity I had carefully crafted—I was forced to confront a question I had never truly asked myself: What is success when there is nothing left to measure?

At first, the loss felt like failure. I had spent years building something only to see it vanish in a matter of months. But then, something unexpected happened. In the silence that followed the storm, I found freedom.

Because when I let go of society's metrics of success, I finally had the space to define my own.

We live in a world that teaches us to measure success in accumulation. More money, more power, more influence, more achievements. And yet, studies show that once basic needs are met, increased wealth and external achievements have little impact on long-term happiness.

What truly fulfills us isn't what we acquire—it's who we become.

Psychologists have found that people who define success by internal growth, relationships, and purpose-driven living report greater life satisfaction and resilience than those who chase external validation.

Letting go of traditional success metrics isn't about giving up ambition—it's about releasing the pressure to perform for the sake of proving something.

And that is exactly what happened to me.

In the wake of my rebirth, after losing nearly everything, I stood at a crossroads. I had two choices:

1. Cling to the past and attempt to rebuild the version of success I once had.

2. Surrender to the unknown and let success find a new meaning in my life.

I chose surrender. And in that surrender, I discovered a truth deeper than any measure of wealth or accolades.

I no longer sought to impress, to prove, or to accumulate. Instead, I lived for self-nurture, self-care, and self-love. My days were no longer dictated by productivity, but by presence. I began to see success not as an outcome, but as a way of being.

And the most shocking part? The moment I stopped chasing success, it started finding me.

Opportunities appeared—not because I forced them, but because I was open to them. Relationships deepened—not because I controlled them, but because I showed up authentically. Life became richer—not because I planned every step, but because I trusted the path.

Success isn't a finish line. It's not an accumulation of mile-stones or the validation of others.

Success is alignment. It is living in a way that feels true to who we are, without the constant weight of expectation.

When we let go of the need to prove ourselves, we find that we already are enough. When we stop measuring life by numbers and titles, we discover that real success is found in meaning, in connection, in presence.

What if success wasn't about what you achieve, but about how fully you live?

In the next section, we'll explore how letting go reclaims our mental and emotional energy, allowing us to live lighter, freer, and with greater peace.

Reclaiming Your Energy

We rarely stop to consider how much mental and emo-tional energy we waste by holding on.

Holding on to old wounds.

Holding on to outdated expectations.

Holding on to narratives that no longer serve us.

We carry the weight of control, gripping tightly to what we think should be, constantly battling reality as it unfolds. And it's exhausting.

Letting go isn't just about surrendering control—it's about reclaiming the energy we've been pouring into resistance.

For months, I felt like I was running in circles—mentally, emotionally, spiritually. I was stuck, exhausted by my own mind.

Halfway through my therapy following my move to Texas, I reached a breaking point. Therapy wasn't working—or at least, that's what I told myself. I felt like I was doing the work, processing the pain, confronting my past. And yet, I was still stuck inside my own suffering.

I remember sitting across from my therapist, hearing her say something I had heard many times before:

"You have to let go."

And I remember my frustration, the way those words landed like an impossible demand.

"Let go of what? Let go how?"

I wasn't clinging on purpose. I wasn't intentionally resisting healing. But I had spent years identifying with my pain, shaping my identity around it. Letting go meant stepping into the unknown, into a version of myself that wasn't built on survival or loss.

That was terrifying.

But at some point, I reached a threshold. I had exhausted every tool in my arsenal—logic, control, analysis, resistance. Nothing was working. So I made a choice.

If letting go was the only way forward, then I would do it fully. No half-measures. No hesitation.

I threw myself into the practice of surrender.

I meditated every morning, even when my thoughts fought me.

I read books that challenged my perception of control.

I surrounded myself with people who embodied ease—people who had mastered the art of flowing with life rather than fighting against it.

One night, everything clicked.

I was sitting under a massive oak tree in downtown Houston, meditating with a group of spiritual healers. I don't know if it was the stillness, the presence of like-minded souls, or the simple willingness to let go, but suddenly, the weight I had been carrying lifted.

I felt light—as if, for the first time in years, I wasn't fighting the current.

The shift wasn't dramatic. There were no fireworks, no grand revelation. Just a quiet, profound realization:

I was free.

Not because life had changed, but because I had stopped gripping so tightly to the past.

Science backs this up. Studies show that letting go of stressors and practicing acceptance leads to lower cortisol levels, improved immune function, and increased emotional resilience.

When we hold on to resistance, we keep our nervous system in a constant state of stress. Our bodies don't know the difference between an immediate threat and an emotional burden we refuse to release. The result? Chronic fatigue, anxiety, and burnout.

But the moment we surrender, our energy shifts.

Instead of fighting life, we align with it. Instead of wasting energy on control, we invest it in presence, creativity, and peace.

I didn't just feel lighter that night under the oak tree. I felt capable. Capable of joy. Capable of love. Capable of stepping into a life that wasn't dictated by the past, but shaped by the freedom of now.

If you feel drained, overwhelmed, or stuck, ask yourself:

What am I gripping too tightly?

What would happen if I released my need to control it?

How much energy would I reclaim if I stopped resisting reality?

The answer may surprise you. Because when we let go, we don't just lose the weight of control—we gain the energy of freedom.

In the next section, we'll explore how letting go transforms relationships, deepening our connections and removing the tension that control so often creates.

Letting Go in Relationships

We often think of love as something we must hold onto tightly, something we must protect, control, and perfect. We fear that if we loosen our grip, if we stop orchestrating every detail, things will fall apart.

But in reality, it is control that suffocates love, not surrender.

The strongest relationships—whether romantic, familial, or professional—are built not on control, but on trust, freedom, and space to grow.

For years, I believed that holding on meant fighting for the people I cared about, ensuring that relationships stayed intact no matter what. I saw compromise as a necessity, sacrifice as a virtue, and conflict as something to be managed, resolved, and controlled.

But love is not a battle to win. It is not a contract to enforce. It is a flow—a connection that must be nurtured, not dictated.

My relationship with Joe was one of the most profound lessons in this truth.

Joe was everything I thought I wanted—committed, passionate, deeply invested in our future. At first, his intensity felt like love itself, like an anchor I could depend on. But over time, it became clear that his needs always took precedence, and I found myself diminishing to accommodate them.

At first, I resisted. I convinced myself that love meant holding on, fixing, proving my worth. I made excuses, adjusted, and clung to the belief that if I just tried harder, things would shift.

They didn't.

The harder I held on, the more the relationship deteriorated. The more I sacrificed myself, the less of me remained.

And then, Joe let go first.

I remember the moment he ended it—the strange mix of heartbreak and relief. I had spent so much energy controlling the outcome, refusing to see what was already lost, that I never realized how free I would feel once the weight of the relationship was gone.

Letting go wasn't losing. It wasn't failure. It was release.

And in that release, I saw clearly for the first time: real love doesn't require us to shrink ourselves to fit into someone else's life.

If control can strangle love, it can also divide families.

For decades, I held onto my anger, my wounds, my history. I carried the weight of old conflicts with my father, the resentment from childhood wounds, and the deeply ingrained belief that letting go meant losing my sense of justice.

I had created a story in my mind—one where I was the victim, where my pain was justified, where the past was a ledger of wrongdoing that could never be erased.

But pain, when held too tightly, becomes an identity. And at some point, I had to ask myself:

Was I holding onto the past because I was still hurt… or because I was afraid of letting it go?

It wasn't easy. Surrendering resentment felt like giving in, like saying everything that happened was okay. But that's not what forgiveness is.

Forgiveness is not about erasing the past. It's about freeing ourselves from being bound by it.

The moment I let go of my grip on my family narrative, something incredible happened. Walls that had stood for years crumbled in an instant. The moment I stopped seeing myself as someone who had been wronged, I saw my father not as a villain, but as a man—a flawed, complicated, deeply human man who had done the best he could with what he had.

And in that moment, I stopped needing to fight.

I let go of the pain, not because it wasn't real, but because I didn't need it anymore. And the result? A family that I once thought was fractured beyond repair became one of my greatest sources of love, connection, and healing.

Control isn't just a burden in personal relationships—it can also poison our professional interactions.

Early in my career, I believed that managing relationships meant controlling them. I thought that collaborations worked best when I dictated the pace, the vision, and the outcome.

But filmmaking taught me something different.

Artists—especially actors—don't thrive under control. They don't respond to rigid expectations and micromanagement. They respond to trust, space, and the freedom to explore.

The moment I stopped trying to steer every detail and instead surrendered to the collaborative process, my productions transformed. Actors, writers, and crew members no longer worked for me; they worked with me. And the results were far better than anything I could have created on my own.

Letting go of control doesn't mean abandoning leadership. It means leading with trust instead of fear.

The truth is, love—whether romantic, familial, or professional—cannot flourish in an environment of control.

To love fully, we must give people the space to be themselves. To trust fully, we must accept that we cannot force outcomes.

Letting go in relationships isn't about walking away—it's about stepping back, making room for growth, and allowing connections to be free, fluid, and real.

Because the strongest relationships aren't the ones we control.

They're the ones we set free.

Now that we've explored how surrender transforms relationships, the next section will capture the essence of letting go through a metaphor that speaks to the heart of surrender.

A Metaphor for Letting Go.

Letting go is not a single moment of release, nor is it an act of surrender that happens all at once. It is a process, a rhythm, a force as natural as the shifting tides or the changing seasons.

If I had to choose an image that encapsulates the experience of surrender, it would be this:

A dandelion releasing its seeds into the wind.

At first glance, the dandelion may seem fragile—its tiny white parachutes light as air, vulnerable to the smallest breath of wind. But in reality, it is one of the most resilient plants in nature.

It doesn't resist the wind.

It doesn't fight to hold on.

It trusts that its seeds will find the right soil, the right conditions, the right time to bloom.

And in that trust, it thrives.

The paradox of surrender is that it often feels like we must do something to let go—as if release requires effort. But true surrender is the opposite of effort.

It is learning to stop gripping so tightly.

It is the unclenching of a fist. The exhale after holding your breath. The moment when you stop pushing upstream and realize the current will carry you exactly where you need to go.

When I think back to my own journey—through loss, reinvention, rebuilding—I see that the times I tried to force life to go my way were the moments I suffered most. It was only when I stopped resisting, when I became like the dandelion, that life flowed effortlessly once again.

Nature is a masterclass in letting go.

The trees don't cling to their leaves in autumn.

The waves don't fight the shore.

The sun doesn't struggle to rise each morning.

They trust the process.

And yet, we—humans, with our complex minds and endless anxieties—constantly resist the flow of life. We hold onto past hurts, outdated dreams, relationships that no longer serve us, careers that drain us, identities that no longer fit.

But just like the tree that trusts its leaves will return in spring, we must trust that what is meant for us will find us.

That what falls away was never meant to stay.

That what remains is what truly belongs.

That life is always guiding us—even when we cannot yet see the destination.

If you're struggling to let go of something right now— whether it's a fear, a past mistake, a relationship, or a dream that no longer fits—ask yourself:

What would happen if I stopped gripping so tightly?

What if I allowed life to carry me, instead of resisting?

Imagine yourself as that dandelion, standing tall in the sunlight, unafraid to release what no longer belongs to you.

Because when you finally let go, you will find that life was always ready to carry you forward.

Letting go is not the end. It is the beginning.

In the next chapter, we will explore how surrender is not just about loss, but about gaining something deeper—a life of peace, authenticity, and profound transformation.

Chapter 5: The Strength in Surrender

Letting go is rarely easy when we're convinced that persistence is the only way forward. The line between perseverance and futility is thin, and when you've invested years of your life into something, surrender can feel like a betrayal of your own efforts. It can feel like failure—until time reveals it was an act of strength all along.

I learned this the hard way in the summer of 2022, eighteen months into developing a business in Austin, Texas. The business was an ambitious venture, built around autonomous robotics—an industry that, at the time, was nowhere near my field of expertise. But I had a vision. And visions don't always wait for credentials. I immersed myself in research, turning late nights into lessons, long drives into opportunities, and business meetings into potential breakthroughs. Houston to Austin became my weekly commute as I pieced together the missing parts of what could be a game-changing company.

The journey was steep and unrelenting, requiring me to learn, adapt, and outwork every obstacle. I found my team—consultants, fund sponsors, a technical co-founder who could bring my vision to life. It was grueling, but I had always been someone who thrived on challenge. And then, without warning, the foundation cracked beneath me.

My technical co-founder, the linchpin of our progress, sat me down one evening and told me he was leaving. Not because he doubted the vision, not because he had lost faith in what we were building, but because he simply couldn't afford to keep going. His father's medical bills had become overwhelming, and an offer from HP in Austin would give him the financial stability he needed. There was no malice, no betrayal—just life, forcing a shift neither of us could control.

I stared at my laptop screen that night, running numbers, creating new strategies, thinking of workarounds. I couldn't accept that this was how it ended. I refused to believe I had come this far just to let it go. But the truth was, without him, the company's trajectory was thrown into limbo. Finding a replacement would take months—months I no longer had. My funding was stretched thin, my resources depleted.

I had a choice. I could keep pushing, knowing that the fight was slipping beyond my grasp, or I could surrender.

For days, I wrestled with the decision. The idea of stopping felt like erasing everything I had built, like admitting to myself that I had wasted a year and a half of relentless effort. But I wasn't naïve. A good businessperson doesn't just know when to build. They also know when to cut their losses.

And so, I did the hardest thing I had ever done: I let go.

I didn't announce it with drama or lament the decision. I simply stopped. I let the dream dissolve into memory and walked away.

At first, it felt like grief. A dull ache in the pit of my stomach, a whisper of what could have been. But over time, that whisper changed. It no longer sounded like failure. It started to sound like wisdom.

In hindsight, surrendering was not weakness—it was self-preservation. It was the acknowledgment that giving something your all does not mean you are obligated to sacrifice yourself for it indefinitely. I had poured my dedication into that company while it was viable, and I had also been wise enough to walk away when it wasn't.

Letting go wasn't defeat. It was a quiet kind of victory—the kind that teaches you your own strength, even when the world doesn't see it.

Psychologists call this "adaptive disengagement"—the ability to recognize when continued effort is counterproductive and to redirect energy toward more viable pursuits. Studies in cognitive psychology suggest that people who can let go of unattainable goals experience lower stress levels and greater overall life satisfaction. Instead of clinging to an idea that is no longer serving them, they shift their focus toward opportunities with higher potential for success.

From a neuroscientific perspective, attachment to control activates the brain's stress response. The amygdala, responsible for processing fear and threat, heightens activity when we perceive loss—whether it's losing a job, a dream, or a relationship. But research has shown that practices like reframing failure as a redirection activate the prefrontal cortex, the rational part of the brain that allows us to regulate emotions and make strategic decisions. In other words, shifting our perspective from loss to opportunity rewires our brain toward resilience rather than despair.

Letting go, then, isn't just a passive act—it's a recalibration of effort. It's recognizing that just because something once felt like the right path, it doesn't mean it always will be.

There's a well-known study in psychological flexibility that shows people who persist too long in impossible tasks experience greater distress than those who adjust their goals. That doesn't mean we should quit at the first sign of difficulty, but it does mean that wisdom lies in knowing when the effort is no longer worth the cost.

Surrendering my company was not a loss of ambition—it was a redirection of it. I wasn't giving up on success; I was making space for it to take a different form. The irony is that the very same resilience that built that company is what allowed me to walk away from it. Because resilience is not just about holding on—it's about knowing when to let go.

Accepting What You Cannot Change

There are moments in life when the sheer force of will is not enough. No matter how much we fight, plead, or plan, reality remains unmoved. These are the moments that test us—not just in strength, but in wisdom. Do we exhaust ourselves in a battle we cannot win, or do we surrender to the truth and find peace in acceptance?

For me, this lesson came in one of the most profound and painful ways: through my father's illness.

When my father suffered a hemorrhage that stripped him of his memories, his independence, and his very sense of self, I refused to believe that this was the end of the man I knew. There was always an answer—there had to be. I consulted with every doctor, researched every treatment, and sought out every possible therapy, convinced that if I just pushed harder, I could reverse the course of his fate.

I was the one making the calls, setting the appointments, seeking opinions from near and far. Each day became a mission. I wasn't just fighting for his life; I was fighting against the very idea that I had no power in this situation. If I stopped trying, what did that mean? That I had failed him? That I had given up?

The problem with refusing to accept reality is that it doesn't change reality—it only prolongs the suffering. And in my relentless pursuit of control, I didn't realize that I was running myself into exhaustion, battling something far beyond my reach.

It was a year into this battle when my father's neurosurgeon asked to meet with me. I knew there was no miraculous breakthrough waiting for me in that room. I had been by my father's side every day—I saw the decline, no matter how much I wanted to deny it. But hearing the doctor speak the words aloud made it real in a way that I had been avoiding.

"There is nothing more you could have done," he told me. "And there is nothing more you can do now."

I drove home that day feeling something strange—a conflict between relief and shame. Relief, because the weight of carrying the impossible had been lifted. Shame, because how could I feel relief in a moment like this? How could I let go when my father was still fighting?

But acceptance isn't about giving up. It's about recognizing when the fight is no longer a fight—it's just suffering. And when we refuse to accept reality, we don't just hurt ourselves. We hurt the people we are trying to save.

The following weeks brought an unexpected shift. I stopped fighting to change the unchangeable, and instead, I focused on being present. Instead of obsessing over new treatments, I sat with him. Instead of searching for solutions, I held his hand. For the first time in a year, I wasn't trying to fix something. I was just there.

One month later, my father passed away.

Looking back, I realize that acceptance wasn't weakness. It was an act of love.

Psychologists talk about radical acceptance—the idea that instead of resisting pain, we acknowledge it for what it is. Studies show that people who practice acceptance experience lower stress levels and greater emotional resilience. Fighting against something we cannot change activates the brain's threat response, keeping us in a cycle of fear and frustration. But when we accept reality, our brain shifts into a state of adaptation, allowing us to move forward instead of remaining stuck in suffering.

I had spent a year trying to fight against life itself, believing that if I just tried hard enough, I could change its course. But life doesn't bend to our will—it moves as it always has, with or without our permission.

What I learned in that year—and in the years that followed—is that acceptance isn't about surrendering to hopelessness. It's about freeing yourself from unnecessary pain.

There are things we can change. There are battles worth fighting. And then there are moments when the only true strength is found in letting go.

When Holding On Hurts More Than Letting Go

From a young age, we are conditioned to associate perseverance with success. Psychologists refer to this as grit, the ability to persist in long-term goals despite setbacks. While grit can be a powerful driver of achievement, research also shows that an unwillingness to let go—even in situations where persistence no longer serves us—can lead to significant mental and physical distress.

Studies in behavioral psychology highlight a phenomenon called "the sunk cost fallacy", where individuals continue investing time, energy, or resources into something simply because they have already committed so much to it. This cognitive bias traps us in situations that no longer serve us, whether it's a failing business, a toxic relationship, or an unrealistic goal. Instead of stepping back and reassessing, we hold on even tighter, believing that letting go would mean failure.

From a neurological perspective, this resistance to letting go is deeply wired into our survival instincts. The brain's limbic system, responsible for processing emotions, reacts strongly to loss—whether it's the loss of a dream, a relationship, or a sense of control. The amygdala, the brain's fear center, perceives surrender as a threat, triggering stress hormones like cortisol and adrenaline. This heightened stress response is linked to anxiety, sleep disturbances, and even cardiovascular disease.

However, emerging research in positive psychology and mindfulness reveals that the ability to surrender—rather than compulsively cling to control—activates the prefrontal cortex, the part of the brain associated with rational thinking and problem-solving. Studies using fMRI scans show that individuals who practice acceptance-based coping strategies exhibit reduced activity in the amygdala and increased activity in regions associated with cognitive flexibility and resilience. In other words, letting go doesn't mean giving up—it means shifting from a state of fear-driven reaction to one of clarity and adaptability.

This is a lesson I had to learn the hard way—through exhaustion, burnout, and the painful realization that control was costing me more than I could afford to give.

One of the most defining moments of my career was the year I ran a classical music festival in Abu Dhabi. It was one of the most prestigious projects I had taken on at that time—a chance to prove myself in a market dominated by multinational players, working alongside world-class musicians, production teams, and international event managers. Every detail had to be perfect, and I made it my mission to ensure that nothing fell apart under my watch.

I oversaw everything: the logistics, the talent arrangements, the client communications, even the minute details backstage and in the hotel rooms. I reviewed every schedule, micromanaged every vendor, triple-checked every itinerary. I lived by the belief that if I was the one in control, then nothing could go wrong.

But things did go wrong.

And when they did, instead of stepping back and trusting the systems in place, I held on even tighter. I inserted myself into every conversation, demanded updates from every department, and burned myself out trying to control the uncontrollable.

I had convinced myself that failure wasn't an option. And when you believe that, you begin to see every minor setback as a catastrophe, every deviation from the plan as a personal defeat.

The festival was a success. The concerts were magnificent. The audience never saw the chaos behind the scenes. But I was wrecked.

By the time the festival ended, I had spent weeks without a proper night's sleep, months running on adrenaline, and days drowning in stress. My body was showing the toll—headaches, digestive issues, constant fatigue. My relationships suffered. My ability to think clearly suffered.

But more than that, I suffered.

Instead of enjoying the achievement, instead of celebrating what had gone right, I could only think about everything that almost went wrong. I had spent so much time trying to keep my grip on everything that I had completely lost my grip on myself.

It wasn't until weeks later—when I finally slowed down enough to breathe—that I realized something crucial:

Holding on so tightly didn't make me stronger. It made me miserable.

There's a reason why holding on to control creates stress, while letting go creates relief. Neuroscientists have found that when we are in a state of chronic control-seeking, our brains remain in a constant state of hypervigilance. The amygdala—the part of the brain responsible for processing fear—becomes overactive, triggering our fight-or-flight response even when there is no real danger.

The result? Anxiety, stress, burnout, and eventually, complete emotional depletion.

On the other hand, when we practice letting go, our brain shifts into a more adaptive state. The prefrontal cortex—the part of the brain responsible for rational thinking and problem-solving—becomes more active, allowing us to see solutions instead of just threats.

This is why people who embrace surrender often experience lower levels of stress hormones (like cortisol), improving problem-solving abilities, greater emotional resilience, and increased creativity and flexibility.

In essence, letting go doesn't just make us feel better—it actually makes us more capable.

Months after the festival ended, I found myself at another crossroad. A new project, a new challenge, and a familiar feeling creeping in—the urge to control, to manage, to perfect.

But this time, I stopped.

I made a conscious decision to step back, trust my team, and allow things to unfold without my constant intervention

And you know what?

Not only did everything go fine, but I also felt a sense of peace that I had never experienced before.

The stress wasn't suffocating. The pressure wasn't unbearable. And for the first time, I saw the power of surrender—not as weakness, but as wisdom.

The world tells us that persistence is the key to success. And sometimes, it is. But not all battles are meant to be fought, and not all struggles are meant to be won.

There is strength in knowing when to walk away.

There is wisdom in knowing when to release your grip.

There is freedom in surrendering to what you cannot change.

And sometimes, the bravest thing you can do is let go.

The Illusion of Control and the Cost of Resistance

We live under the illusion that control equals security. That if we plan enough, work hard enough, and anticipate every possible outcome, we can prevent life's worst-case scenarios. This belief is comforting—it gives us a sense of agency in an unpredictable world. But reality is far less cooperative. Life moves according to its own rhythms, indifferent to our best-laid plans.

For years, I operated under the belief that I could anticipate, prevent, and shape every outcome in my life. It wasn't arrogance—just an ingrained survival strategy. I had convinced myself that if I just put in enough effort, strategized well enough, and stayed disciplined, I could carve my own fate. I learned the mechanics of control early in life, watching those around me succeed or fail based on how well they played their hands. The rules seemed clear: work harder than everyone else, never show weakness, and always be one step ahead.

This belief served me well—until it didn't.

The human brain is wired to seek predictability because uncertainty triggers a threat response. A study published in Nature Communications found that uncertainty about future outcomes activates the anterior cingulate cortex, a region linked to anxiety and distress. In other words, when we feel out of control, our brains interpret it as danger—even if no real threat exists.

This is why we grasp at control so tightly. We micromanage relationships, plan careers decades in advance, obsess over financial security, and even try to control how others perceive us. The problem is, life doesn't conform to our scripts. People change, economies shift, opportunities vanish, and health fluctuates. And the more we resist these changes, the more we suffer.

One of the clearest examples of this in my life was when I was building my company in Mexico City. I had invested not just money, but my entire sense of purpose into making it succeed. The idea of failure was unthinkable. I had structured everything—operations, partnerships, even contingency plans—to ensure that things would run smoothly. But when my co-founder decided to step back from the business, everything unraveled.

At first, I refused to accept it. I tried persuasion, renegotiation, and restructuring. I spent months convincing myself that if I just found the right workaround, I could get things back on track. The sheer mental exhaustion of clinging to a situation that was slipping through my fingers was unlike anything I had experienced before.

Psychologists call this "emotional labor"—the exhausting process of maintaining an illusion. Holding onto a version of reality that no longer exists is like carrying a weight that grows heavier by the day. The deeper we entrench ourselves in resistance, the more we strain our emotional and cognitive resources. Studies show that chronic stress from control struggles contributes to decision fatigue, burnout, and even compromised immune function.

It wasn't until I surrendered—fully and honestly—that I saw things for what they were. The business wasn't viable under its original vision. My co-founder had made a choice that was right for him. And I had a choice too: to keep fighting against reality or to accept the truth and move forward.

At the time, I couldn't accept the truth. My only reaction was to walk away—like one walks away from a broken relationship, unwilling to process the full weight of the betrayal just yet. I told myself things couldn't get worse, that I needed time alone to deal with what felt like an emotional and professional breakup. I felt abandoned, unfairly treated by someone who was supposed to be my partner, my anchor in a country where I was never a citizen. I wouldn't have started a company there if not for his promise to stand beside me every step of the way, if he hadn't shared my vision and encouraged me to build something from the ground up. His sudden withdrawal felt not just like a business setback, but a personal betrayal.

At first, I thought I had been foolish to trust, naive to believe that commitments were unbreakable and that loyalty meant the same thing to everyone. But in the quiet months that followed, as life unraveled in ways I never could have predicted, I came to understand that my anger toward my co-founder had little to do with his decision itself—it was about what it represented to me. His choice to scale back his engagement in our company felt like a disregard for my vision, a dismissal of my relentless effort to stay in control. He had pulled the carpet from under my feet, leaving me exposed to uncertainty, and in that moment, I equated his choice with betrayal.

But with time and distance, I saw it differently. The truth was, I had been sacrificing my personal comfort to protect a business plan, as if my devotion to structure and persistence alone could guarantee happiness. He, on the other hand, had chosen himself over an agreement—something I had failed to do for myself. At first, I resented him for it. But after experiencing my own upheavals, I came to respect his decision more than my reaction to it. He wasn't reckless or disloyal—he was simply honest about his limits. And perhaps, the greater mistake was mine: believing that control, rather than adaptability, was what truly mattered.

It was months later that I saw the truth: it wasn't the loss itself that had devastated me—it was my refusal to accept it. My energy had been drained not by the events themselves, but by my resistance to them. I had spent months replaying conversations, analyzing what I could have done differently, holding on to the illusion that if I had just controlled things better, none of this would have happened. But the world doesn't work that way.

The paradox is that true power comes not from controlling, but from releasing. When we let go, we reclaim the energy that was wasted on resistance. We stop running in circles and start moving forward.

This realization changed the way I approached every challenge after that. I no longer asked, How do I stop this from happening? Instead, I asked, What is this moment trying to show me?

Because the truth is, life doesn't punish us with change. It invites us to grow through it.

Accepting What You Cannot Change: The Path to Inner Freedom

There is a quiet agony in resisting the inevitable. The mind spins endless narratives, searching for ways to undo the past or force a future that isn't meant to be. We replay conversations, rewrite choices, and tell ourselves that if we had just tried a little harder, fought a little longer, or controlled things a little better, the outcome would have been different. This mental resistance, this refusal to accept what is, is the source of immense suffering.

For a long time, I lived in this struggle. I believed that if I exerted enough effort, I could prevent life's harsher realities. I could protect the people I loved, control my circumstances, and guarantee outcomes. But life is not an equation where effort always equals reward. It is wild, unpredictable, and often indifferent to our best-laid plans.

This truth became painfully clear to me when my father fell ill. His sudden decline shattered the illusion that I could shield those I loved from suffering. At first, I fought against reality with everything I had. I sought out the best doctors, researched experimental treatments, and traveled across cities looking for answers that didn't exist. I told myself that as long as I kept moving, as long as I didn't stop searching, I could find a way to restore him. To fix things. To make them right.

But there came a day when I had to face the truth. The doctor overseeing his case sat me down and gently told me what I already knew in my heart but refused to accept: I had done everything possible, and it would not be enough. The weight of those words settled in my chest like a stone. For so long, I had been running—not just from the reality of his condition, but from the deeper truth that I was never in control to begin with.

Leaving that conversation, I felt something shift. A strange, uneasy calm settled over me. I wasn't relieved, exactly, but the weight of resistance had lifted. I had been fighting a battle that was never mine to win, exhausting myself in the process. And now, finally, I was allowing life to unfold as it would.

There is a profound lesson in this: when we accept what we cannot change, we do not become powerless—we become free. We free ourselves from the torment of "what if" and step into the reality of what is. Acceptance is not giving up. It is not passivity. It is the conscious decision to stop expending energy on battles that cannot be won and instead direct that energy toward healing, toward presence, toward peace.

Psychologists call this radical acceptance—the practice of fully acknowledging reality without judgment or resistance. Research shows that those who embrace radical acceptance experience lower levels of stress and anxiety, improved mental health, and a greater sense of inner peace. A study published in Clinical Psychology Review found that individuals who practiced acceptance-based coping strategies showed significantly lower rates of depression and emotional distress than those who engaged in avoidance or denial.

This is because resistance amplifies suffering. When we resist, we trap ourselves in a loop of frustration, trying to control what cannot be controlled. But when we surrender to reality, we allow ourselves to move forward. We redirect our energy toward things that matter—toward healing, adaptation, and resilience.

In the months following my father's passing, I saw this truth reflected in other areas of my life. The need to control, to force things into place, had not just consumed me in this one instance—it had been the backdrop of my entire existence. I had spent years chasing certainty, believing that my plans and efforts could safeguard me from disappointment, loss, and failure. But real security doesn't come from controlling life. It comes from knowing that, no matter what happens, you will find a way through.

Acceptance is not a single moment of clarity, nor is it a switch that, once flipped, frees us from suffering forever. It is a practice—one we must choose again and again, sometimes daily, sometimes hourly. There are days when surrender feels natural, when we meet life's difficulties with grace, allowing them to flow through us rather than fighting against them. And then there are days when we resist with everything in us, clinging to what we wish things could be, wrestling with the illusion that if we just try harder, we can make reality conform to our will.

The battle is often subtle. It doesn't always come in the form of dramatic life events or earth-shattering losses. Sometimes, it is the quiet tension in our bodies when things don't go as planned. The simmering frustration when the universe does not unfold according to our time-lines. The resentment we hold toward those who made choices we wish they hadn't. The ache of unmet expecta-tions, unfulfilled dreams, and the gap between what we wanted and what *is*.

This is where the real work of surrender happens. Not in a grand, cinematic moment of enlightenment, but in the small, daily choices we make to loosen our grip—to trust that even in uncertainty, we are exactly where we need to be. It is in the decision to breathe through disappointment rather than letting it consume us. In the quiet understand-ing that we do not have to have all the answers. In the will-ingness to let go of narratives that no longer serve us and embrace the unknown with an open heart.

Spiritually, acceptance is the ultimate act of faith. It is the willingness to believe that there is meaning even when we do not yet understand it. That our pain has purpose, that our losses are not voids but transitions, that the universe is not conspiring against us but guiding us toward something greater—something we cannot yet see. Many spiritual tra-ditions teach that suffering is not caused by pain itself, but by our resistance to it. In Buddhism, attachment is said to be the root of all suffering—our attachment to how things *should* be, to what we *deserve*, to the belief that life must unfold according to our script. But when we surrender, we break free from these attachments. We move from resis-tance to trust, from control to flow, from fear to freedom.

And in that release, we find something we never expected: peace. Not the peace that comes from things going our way, but the deeper, unshakable peace that comes from knowing that no matter what happens, we will find a way through. A peace that is not dependent on external circumstances but rooted in the quiet strength of knowing that we do not need to fight life—we can move with it. We can embrace the unknown, sit with discomfort, and allow change to shape us rather than break us.

This is the kind of peace that transforms us. Not a passive resignation, but an active surrender—a choice to trust that life, in all its unpredictability, is unfolding as it should.

Letting Go of Ego

Ego is a fortress we build to protect ourselves. It gives us an identity, a sense of importance, and the illusion of control. It whispers that we are defined by our accomplishments, our titles, our reputations. It convinces us that letting go is weakness, that surrender is failure. But what happens when the fortress becomes a prison?

I had spent much of my life curating an identity—one I could present to the world with confidence. Success was not just a goal; it was the foundation of my self-worth. I needed to be seen as accomplished, capable, and in control. It wasn't arrogance—it was survival. The world rewarded those who had their act together, and I had trained myself to fit that mold. But over time, I realized that the identity I had crafted was also my greatest limitation.

One of the hardest lessons I ever learned was that being right is not the same as being free. There were times I clung to my perspective, my way of doing things, simply because admitting otherwise felt like losing a battle. But surrender is not about losing. It's about choosing something greater than pride—it's about choosing peace.

I remember a time early in my career when I was invited to a prestigious event as a writer. It was a moment that should have felt validating, proof that I had carved out a space for myself in the world. But something felt off. At the time, I saw myself as one thing—a writer. I had built an entire persona around it. So when someone asked, "What else do you do?" I resisted the question. I didn't want to be anything else. I was attached to the identity I had worked so hard to establish.

Years later, I would look back and realize that my resistance had been fear in disguise. The fear of being undefined, of stepping outside of the identity that gave me value. But the truth is, identity should be fluid. The moment I allowed myself to expand beyond labels, I discovered more freedom than I had ever known.

Ego convinces us that we are the sum of our accomplishments, that our worth is measured by what we do, what we own, and how others perceive us. It tells us that letting go—of plans, of expectations, of tightly held identities—is dangerous because without them, who are we? But true wisdom reveals the opposite: it is not in clinging that we find ourselves, but in releasing.

For most of our lives, we wear masks, consciously or unconsciously curating identities that fit the narratives we believe will bring us love, respect, or validation. We chase success, thinking it will give us meaning. We define ourselves by our roles, believing they make us valuable. And we grip tightly to the story we tell about who we are, fearful that if we let go, we will dissolve into nothingness. But the paradox is this: the more we attach to an identity, the more we limit ourselves. A river does not cease to exist when it changes course—it simply finds a new way forward.

The ancient wisdom of many spiritual traditions teaches that we suffer not because life is cruel, but because we resist its natural flow. In Buddhism, attachment is the root of suffering; in Kabbalah, clinging to a rigid sense of self prevents us from aligning with divine energy. In every mystical tradition, there is a call to surrender—to release what is false so that we may embrace what is real.

So what is real?

Real is the presence beneath the mask. It is the part of us that remains when titles, successes, and labels are stripped away. It is the silent awareness that does not need to prove itself, because it simply is. The moment we stop fearing the loss of control, we make space for something greater: freedom. Not freedom that comes from power, status, or external validation, but the kind that comes from no longer needing any of it to feel whole.

Imagine a clenched fist, holding tightly onto something small, something fragile. The tighter we grip, the more it crumbles in our hands. But when we open our palms, when we release, we are no longer confined by what we were trying to hold onto—we are free to receive whatever life is offering next. That is the wisdom of letting go: the knowing that we are never losing ourselves, but always discovering a deeper truth.

To surrender the ego is not to lose—it is to return to something we have always been but have long forgotten. It is stepping out of the illusion of control and stepping into the vastness of what is.

We spend much of our lives chasing validation—proving to the world that we are successful, worthy, important, enough. But what happens when we step away from that pursuit? What remains of us?

The greatest act of strength is not in proving ourselves to others. It is in realizing we never had to.

There is an illusion we are sold—that strength is loud, visible, and commanding. That it is measured in how much we achieve, how many people recognize our greatness, how well we outperform expectations. But real strength, the kind that transforms lives, is quieter than that. It does not shout; it does not demand. It simply exists. It is the unwavering confidence that comes from knowing that our worth was never dependent on external proof.

To arrive at that place—to stand in your truth without needing an audience—is a liberation unlike any other. It is the difference between striving and being. Between running toward an illusion and standing fully present in who you already are.

In letting go of the need to prove, we reclaim the energy once spent on performance. We stop contorting ourselves into shapes we were never meant to be, just to fit into spaces that were never meant for us. And in that release, we discover a life not driven by approval but by authenticity.

This is where peace begins—not in accomplishment, but in the quiet knowing that who we are, as we are, is already enough.

Spiritual Surrender: The Deepest Letting Go

To surrender spiritually is to recognize that we are part of something vast, something beyond comprehension. It is to let go of the illusion that we must figure everything out on our own. It is to step into the flow of life, rather than constantly swimming against it.

This idea of surrender is echoed across spiritual traditions and philosophical teachings, revealing a universal truth: the greatest wisdom is found not in resistance, but in alignment with the natural flow of life. In the ancient Chinese text, the Tao Te Ching, Lao Tzu describes this state as wu wei—effortless action, the art of flowing with life rather than struggling against it. Wu wei is not passivity; it is the profound understanding that life has its own current, and when we stop trying to force our way upstream, we allow ourselves to be carried toward something far greater than our limited minds could conceive.

Lao Tzu teaches, "When I let go of what I am, I become what I might be." This surrender is not about abandoning responsibility or relinquishing ambition; it is about softening our grip on the rigid identities and expectations that keep us trapped. We often cling to our roles, our titles, our carefully constructed versions of ourselves, believing that they define us. But in doing so, we leave no room for growth, no space for transformation. The paradox of life is that only in letting go do we make room for something new to emerge.

In Buddhism, this principle manifests as anicca—impermanence. Everything in life is in constant motion, shifting, evolving. To resist change is to invite suffering, because suffering arises not from change itself, but from our attachment to what we wish would stay the same. The Buddha taught that freedom comes from recognizing this impermanence and surrendering to it with grace. When we stop fearing change and instead embrace it as part of the natural order, we free ourselves from the anxiety of the unknown.

The Bhagavad Gita, one of Hinduism's most revered scriptures, presents another dimension of surrender—Ishvarapranidhana, or devotion to the divine. Krishna tells Arjuna, "Abandon all attachment to the results of your actions and take refuge in me." This does not mean inaction; rather, it calls for acting with full presence and effort while releasing attachment to the outcome. This is the essence of surrender—not passivity, but trust. Trust that we are where we need to be. Trust that our efforts are not in vain. Trust that the unfolding of life is wiser than our grasping for certainty.

Even in Western philosophy, we find echoes of this truth. The Stoics, particularly Epictetus and Marcus Aurelius, spoke of surrender in terms of amor fati—the love of fate. Marcus Aurelius wrote, "Accept whatever comes to you woven in the pattern of your destiny, for what could more aptly fit your needs?" This is not the same as resignation; it is a radical acceptance that whatever life brings is neither good nor bad in itself—it is only our resistance that creates suffering. The Stoics believed that peace is found not in controlling life, but in mastering our response to it.

All of these traditions—Taoism, Buddhism, Hinduism, Stoicism—point toward the same realization: true surrender is not giving up. It is stepping into the current of life, trusting its wisdom, and allowing it to guide us toward who we are meant to become. It is the shift from control to flow, from resistance to presence, from fear to faith.

To surrender is to trust that life knows what it is doing. And when we learn to let go, we do not lose ourselves—we find the vastness of what we were always meant to be..

Some people experience this surrender through religion, others through nature, through meditation, through silence. It is the moment we stop asking, Why is this happening to me? and start asking, What is this here to teach me? It is the moment we release our grip on outcomes and trust that even in uncertainty, there is a path unfolding.

In Jewish mysticism, the concept of *bitachon*—deep trust in divine providence—mirrors this truth in a way that challenges our deepest fears and attachments. *Bitachon* is not a passive resignation to fate, nor is it blind optimism that everything will unfold exactly as we wish. It is something far more profound: an unshakable inner knowing that even in the midst of life's greatest uncertainties, there is meaning, there is order, and there is a guiding presence moving through it all.

The Baal Shem Tov, founder of Hasidic Judaism, taught that every experience, no matter how painful or confusing, is an invitation to recognize the hidden hand of the divine.

Nothing in our lives is accidental. Even our losses, our struggles, and our darkest moments are woven into a greater design, one we may not yet be able to see. The challenge is not to avoid hardship, but to trust that even within hardship, there is something unfolding that is ultimately for our highest good.

This teaching is deeply connected to the idea of *hashgacha pratis*—divine providence in every detail of existence. The Baal Shem Tov emphasized that nothing, not even the falling of a single leaf from a tree, happens outside the will of the divine. Every moment is intentional. Every twist in our path, every delay, every heartbreak, every unexpected turn is not a deviation but a redirection. The question is not *why is this happening to me?* but *what is this moment asking of me?*

Consider the story of Rabbi Akiva, one of the greatest sages of Jewish history. It is told that he was once traveling and sought shelter in a village, but every door was closed to him. Forced to spend the night in the wilderness, he had with him a donkey, a rooster, and a lantern. In the night, a strong wind blew out his lantern, a wild animal devoured his rooster, and his donkey was stolen. To any ordinary person, this would have seemed like an endless string of misfortunes. Yet Rabbi Akiva responded with one simple phrase: *"Everything that God does is for the good."*

The next morning, he discovered that during the night, a band of thieves had raided the village that had refused him shelter. Had his lantern been lit, had his rooster crowed, had his donkey brayed, he would have been discovered and captured. What appeared to be loss was, in fact, protection. What seemed to be misfortune was, in truth, divine intervention.

This is the essence of *bitachon*—the radical trust that even when life does not make sense, even when things seem to be falling apart, there is a wisdom greater than ours at play. It does not mean we will always be spared suffering.

It does not mean we will always get what we want. It means that even in the moments that shake us to our core, we can trust that we are being held.

The Zohar, the foundational text of Jewish mysticism, speaks of this trust as the act of surrendering our limited perception to the infinite wisdom of the divine. It teaches that our perspective is like that of a person standing beneath a vast tapestry, seeing only a tangled mess of threads, while above, the full masterpiece is revealed. Our job is not to understand every detail but to trust that the design exists.

Even in chaos, there is purpose. Even in darkness, there is light waiting to be revealed. The Talmud states, *"Just as we bless the good, so too must we bless the bad."* This is not a call to pretend suffering does not exist, nor is it an invitation to suppress grief. Rather, it is the recognition that sometimes what seems like an ending is only the beginning of a transformation we cannot yet comprehend.

To embrace *bitachon* is to release our grip on the need to control every outcome. It is to step forward in faith, knowing that even when the path is unclear, even when we feel lost, we are still being guided. And that trust—more than any plan, more than any illusion of control—is what gives us the strength to keep walking.

I have seen this surrender in people who have lost everything and still found a way forward. I have seen it in those who, instead of being crushed by hardship, have softened into it, allowing themselves to be carried rather than consumed. I have felt it in my own moments of deepest despair, when the only option left was to trust that life had not abandoned me, that even in my losses, there was something waiting to be found.

Spiritual surrender does not mean we stop acting. It does not mean we become passive, letting life happen to us. It means we meet life with open hands instead of clenched fists. It means we walk our path without needing to control where every step leads.

There is a reason so many wisdom traditions use water as a metaphor for surrender. Water does not resist—it flows. It bends around obstacles, carves through mountains, finds its way through even the smallest openings. It does not grasp or demand, yet it is powerful beyond measure. When we stop resisting, when we trust the currents of our own lives, we move with the same quiet strength.

And in that surrender, we find something we were searching for all along—peace. Not the kind that comes from certainty, but the kind that comes from knowing we never needed certainty to begin with.

Fear of the unknown is one of the deepest human anxieties. We are wired to seek certainty, to map out the future as best we can, to find security in predictability. But life, in its infinite wisdom, does not offer certainty—it offers movement, evolution, and change. The more we try to grip tightly to what we know, the more life nudges us forward, asking us to step into the unknown.

This is why surrender is not passive—it is courageous. It requires us to release our need for guarantees, to step forward even when we cannot see the ground beneath our feet. It is the moment when we say, "I do not know what comes next, but I trust that I will find my way."

In Kabbalistic teachings, there is a phrase often repeated in moments of uncertainty: Lech Lecha—"Go forth." It was the command given to Abraham when he was told to leave everything familiar behind and walk toward an unknown destiny. The words do not come with a map or a destination; they simply mean go. Walk in faith, even when you do not understand. Trust that the path will reveal itself as you move forward.

This idea is not unique to Jewish thought. In Buddhism, the concept of impermanence teaches that clinging to what is known is the root of suffering. Everything in life is in constant motion—the seasons change, people change, circumstances evolve. When we resist this natural flow, we create suffering. When we embrace it, we find liberation.

The same wisdom appears in the Hindu Bhagavad Gita, where Krishna tells Arjuna: You have the right to your actions, but not to the fruits of your actions. In other words, do your part, give your best effort, but let go of the need to control the outcome.

Letting go of control does not mean we stop dreaming, planning, or acting. It means we release the belief that we must know exactly where life is leading us. It is the shift from I must control everything to I will walk forward with trust.

I have seen this surrender in my own life. There were moments when the future was entirely unknown—when a plan fell apart, a business collapsed, a relationship ended, or a door I expected to open remained shut. I fought against those moments, believing I had failed, believing I had lost something. But looking back, I see that every unknown I was forced to step into led me somewhere I never could have planned. Some of the best things in my life were not the result of meticulous strategy, but of allowing life to take me where I was meant to go.

Surrendering to the unknown is not about passivity. It is about participation. It is about saying yes to life, even when we do not have all the answers. It is about meeting uncertainty with curiosity instead of fear. It is about knowing that, no matter where the road leads, we will be okay—not because we are in control, but because we are always supported in ways we cannot yet see.

When we embrace the unknown, we step into the fullest expression of who we are meant to be. Because certainty does not lead to growth—uncertainty does. And when we surrender to it, we allow life to unfold in ways more beautiful than we could have ever imagined.

Surrender as Strength: The Power of Softness in a Hard World

In a world that glorifies resilience as toughness, we are taught to equate strength with resistance. We are told to stand firm, push back, fight for control. But true strength is not rigidity—it is adaptability. It is not found in unyielding resistance but in the ability to bend without breaking.

Water is often used as a metaphor for surrender in many spiritual traditions. The Tao Te Ching describes water as the softest yet most powerful force in nature. It does not resist obstacles; it moves around them. It does not try to overpower; it simply flows. And in doing so, it carves mountains, shapes landscapes, and wears down even the hardest stone.

This is the essence of true surrender—not weakness, but the wisdom to flow with life instead of exhausting ourselves fighting against it.

I used to believe that surrender meant defeat. That if I stopped pushing, if I stopped trying to control every outcome, I would lose. But life, with its quiet lessons, kept showing me otherwise. The moments when I let go, when I stopped resisting what was happening and instead embraced it, those were the moments that gave me real strength.

I once met a Rabbi at a meditation retreat who was blind. She was not there to overcome her blindness, to fight against it, or to search for ways to compensate for what she lacked. She was there simply to be—to experience, to meditate, to connect. At first, I found myself focused on the ways she had to navigate differently. I wanted to ensure she had all the assistance she needed, that she wasn't missing anything. But over the days, I realized she wasn't the one struggling—I was. I was the one who saw her as needing something, as being limited in some way. She, on the other hand, was immersed, like the rest of us, in exploring deeper layers of meditation and self-discovery. She had long surrendered to what is. She had stopped seeing her condition as something to resist, something to overcome, something that defined her. Instead, she simply lived in harmony with her reality, unburdened by the need to change what could not be changed.

That kind of surrender is rare. It is the ability to fully accept what is without bitterness, without regret, without the desperate attempt to force life into something else. She was not struggling against her blindness—she had embraced it. And in doing so, she was more free than many of us who were still clinging to our illusions of control.

There is strength in that kind of surrender. The kind that does not seek to dominate life but to dance with it. The kind that does not see loss or limitation as failure but as part of the natural rhythm of existence.

We are so conditioned to believe that if we soften, if we release control, we will be swept away. But what if the opposite is true? What if surrender is what allows us to stand taller, to move forward with greater ease, to meet life with open hands instead of clenched fists?

The hardest lessons in my life were the ones that demanded surrender. They were the moments that broke me open, that forced me to let go of everything I thought I needed in order to see what was truly mine. And in every case, surrender did not weaken me—it made me stronger. More resilient. More at peace.

Because strength is not in how hard we fight. It is in how well we let go.

Chapter 6: The Strength in Vulnerability

The Illusion of Self-Sufficiency

We are taught to believe that independence is a virtue, that self-sufficiency is the highest form of strength. From a young age, I learned to rely on myself, not out of choice, but out of necessity. In my family, interdependence wasn't encouraged—competition was. My parents reinforced the idea that survival meant standing on your own two feet, and that reliance on others was a dangerous weakness. I saw firsthand how promises of help could evaporate when things got tough. My father, a businessman, had trusted business partners, only to see them abandon their responsibilities and fail him when times got hard. The lesson was clear: You are what you have, and if you have nothing, you are nothing.

For years, this belief shaped how I moved through the world. I carried my burdens alone, convinced that strength meant never asking for help. I worked tirelessly, determined to never be caught in a position where I had to depend on anyone. And yet, life has a way of breaking down even the most rigid beliefs.

I remember during my sophomore year at Notre Dame, I was living with four roommates in a two-bedroom flat. We all came from the same high school, though from different classes, so we weren't particularly close at first. I had no car, so I walked to class and relied on public transportation to get to a job I had at a skating arena a few miles away. One day, I was on the phone with someone I was dating on campus, and she suggested we go to a concert that weekend. I felt trapped. I didn't have a car, I couldn't afford to rent one, and I had no idea how to make it work.

I had spent my entire life believing that if I couldn't do something on my own, then I simply couldn't do it. I would have rather canceled the date, made up an excuse, or found another way to get there alone than admit I needed help. But that day, one of my roommates overheard my frustration. He was two years my senior, and without hesitation, he offered me his car for the weekend.

I couldn't believe it. It felt unnatural to accept. I hesitated, tried to politely decline, but he insisted. "Just ask when you need something," he told me.

That moment changed me. For the first time, I realized that my belief in radical self-sufficiency had been a prison. I had spent years thinking that needing help made me weak, that asking for support meant I was failing in some way. But accepting that offer didn't make me weak. It made me human.

That weekend wasn't just about having a car. It was about realizing that people could be there for me if I let them. My relationship with that roommate, with my other roommates, and with people in general changed after that. I learned that strength isn't in isolation—it's in connection. That moment cracked open a door in my life that had been shut for too long. It taught me that true strength lies in knowing when to stand alone and when to lean on others.

For years, I had carried my father's lesson like a shield, believing that my worth was measured by what I could carry on my own. But in that moment, I began to understand a deeper truth: Strength is not about having no needs. It is about knowing that when you do, you don't have to face them alone.

Breaking Down the Walls

For most of my life, vulnerability felt like a dangerous gamble. It was something to be avoided, something that made you too exposed, too easy to hurt. I had learned early on that keeping things to myself was safer—that maintaining a sense of control over my emotions and failures meant I could protect my reputation, my ambitions, my sense of self.

But the truth is, walls don't just keep people out. They also keep us locked inside.

There was a moment early in my entrepreneurial journey when I made a choice that felt completely counterintuitive at the time—I admitted failure publicly. I had spent months working on a business idea, pouring everything into it, only to realize that it wasn't gaining traction. Investors weren't biting, the market wasn't responding, and I was at a crossroads.

My instincts told me to keep quiet, to pivot behind the scenes, to make sure that no one saw me struggling. The last thing I wanted was for people to think I wasn't capable, that I didn't know what I was doing. But at the same time, I was exhausted. The weight of keeping up appearances, of pretending like things were fine when they weren't, was heavier than the failure itself.

So, in a moment of honesty, I did something I had never done before—I shared my failure openly. I wrote a candid post detailing what went wrong, the mistakes I had made, and the lessons I had learned. I expected criticism. I expected judgment. Maybe even some whispers of, "I knew he wasn't going to make it."

But what I got was the exact opposite.

People didn't mock me. They related to me. Entrepreneurs I admired reached out to share their own failures, their own near-misses, their own struggles that no one had seen from the outside. Instead of damaging my credibility, my honesty strengthened it. Instead of losing connections, I gained them.

That moment changed the way I saw vulnerability—not as a weakness, but as a bridge. It deepened my relationships, made me more relatable, and actually strengthened my reputation. People didn't see me as the guy who failed; they saw me as the guy who learns, adapts, and keeps going.

The hardest part wasn't dealing with the response—it was pressing "publish." It was allowing myself to be seen, unguarded, without the armor of certainty. Every instinct told me to maintain the illusion of control. But what I gained—authentic connections, unexpected opportunities, and a stronger sense of self—proved that real strength isn't in never falling. It's in being honest enough to say, "Here's what happened. Here's what I learned. And here's what's next."

Breaking down the walls isn't easy. It requires undoing years of conditioning that tells us to be strong, to be self-sufficient, to always have it together. But the moment we let those walls crack, we allow light to come in. We allow others to meet us where we are, instead of where we pretend to be.

And in doing so, we realize that we were never meant to do it alone.

The Power of Saying "I Don't Know"

For most of my life, I believed that competence was measured by certainty. Strength, I thought, lay in always having an answer, a solution, a plan. Whether in business, leadership, or personal life, I felt that knowing what to do at all times was not just an expectation, but a necessity. To admit uncertainty felt like admitting failure, like exposing a vulnerability that could unravel everything I had built.

This belief wasn't just a personal philosophy—it was deeply ingrained in our culture. From an early age, we are conditioned to believe that intelligence is about having the right answers, that leadership is about unwavering confidence, and that doubt is a weakness. But science tells a different story.

In cognitive psychology, the Dunning-Kruger effect describes how people with limited knowledge often overestimate their expertise, while those who are truly competent recognize the vastness of what they don't know. The more knowledgeable you become, the more aware you are of the complexities and uncertainties of the world. Ironically, admitting I don't know is often a sign of wisdom, not ignorance.

Another study published in Psychological Science found that people who embrace intellectual humility—acknowledging their own limitations and gaps in knowledge—tend to make better decisions, solve problems more effectively, and foster stronger relationships. Leaders who display intellectual humility create environments where collaboration thrives, where diverse perspectives are valued, and where true innovation can take place.

But I didn't always understand this.

There was a pivotal moment in my career when I found myself leading a project that was quickly unraveling. I had navigated high-pressure situations before, always finding ways to push through. But this time, every strategy I attempted failed. The more I tried to assert control, the more the situation slipped through my fingers.

At first, I resisted the truth. I poured over data, dissected every possible angle, and convinced myself that if I just worked harder, I would figure it out. But nothing changed. The weight of responsibility grew heavier, and the fear of admitting that I didn't have the answers became suffocating.

The stress of that moment was not just psychological—it was physiological. Neuroscientists have found that uncertainty activates the anterior cingulate cortex, the region of the brain associated with conflict detection and cognitive effort. When we feel out of control, our brains interpret it as a threat, triggering the amygdala, which governs our fight-or-flight response. This reaction can lead to decision paralysis, where fear of making the wrong choice prevents us from making any choice at all.

I was caught in that cycle—unable to move forward, yet unwilling to admit I was stuck.

Then, in a moment of exhaustion and frustration, I did something completely against my instincts—I admitted the truth. I told my team that I didn't have the answer, that I was struggling to find the right way forward.

What happened next changed everything.

Instead of losing faith in me, my team responded with relief. Some of them had sensed the roadblocks but had been hesitant to speak up, assuming I had it under control. The moment I acknowledged my uncertainty, the conversation shifted. People opened up. New ideas surfaced. The weight I had been carrying alone suddenly became something we all held together.

In that moment, I saw with absolute clarity: Leadership is not about having all the answers—it's about creating the space for solutions to emerge.

This realization is supported by research from Harvard Business School, which found that leaders who acknowledge their limitations and invite input from their teams foster greater trust, higher engagement, and more innovative problem-solving. The strongest leaders aren't the ones who pretend to know everything; they're the ones who make it safe for others to contribute their expertise.

The irony is that by admitting I don't know, I didn't lose credibility—I gained it. My team didn't see me as weak; they saw me as honest, as someone who valued truth over ego. It built trust in a way that pretending never could.

In retrospect, that moment was a turning point. Surrendering to uncertainty didn't just open doors—it brought new perspectives, new collaborators, and unexpected opportunities that I never would have encountered if I had clung to the illusion of control.

We are conditioned to believe that certainty is strength. But in reality, certainty can be a cage. It keeps us locked in rigid thinking, afraid to explore, afraid to question, afraid to change. Growth happens when we embrace uncertainty, when we allow curiosity to replace fear, when we surrender to the fact that not knowing is not a weakness—it is an invitation to discover.

Saying I don't know is not the end of competence. It is the beginning of wisdom. It is the space where true innovation, creativity, and transformation happen.

And the moment I embraced that, I stopped fearing uncertainty. Instead, I started seeing it for what it truly was: possibility.

Learning to Receive

We often hear that it is better to give than to receive, but what happens when giving is all we allow ourselves to do? The culture of self-reliance glorifies independence, teaching us that strength means standing alone, that needing help is a sign of weakness. This narrative is deeply ingrained in our psyche, shaping how we interact with the world and perceive ourselves.

But there comes a time when life humbles us, when the facade of invulnerability cracks, and we are left with no choice but to lean on others. These are the moments that test our true strength—not in our capacity to endure alone but in our willingness to admit that we can't.

Growing up, I was taught that self-reliance was the ultimate goal. The lessons of my childhood, embedded in sayings like "You are what you have in your pocket. If you have a dollar, you are worth a dollar," cultivated a mindset that equated self-worth with financial independence and personal capability. Independence became my armor, a shield against the vulnerabilities of needing anyone else.

The problem with this kind of thinking is that it isolates us from the very connections that sustain and enrich our lives. Studies in psychology suggest that hyper-independence, often rooted in past experiences of betrayal or disappointment, can lead to emotional burnout and social isolation. Researchers have found that individuals who resist seeking help are more likely to suffer from chronic stress, anxiety, and even depression. The effort to maintain an image of strength becomes a source of constant internal conflict, depleting our mental and emotional resources.

One of the most profound shifts in my life came when I hit rock bottom in Texas. Stripped of financial security, direction, and, quite frankly, my will to keep moving forward, I found myself at the mercy of circumstances I could not control. My instinct was to muscle through it alone, clinging to the illusion that I was strong enough to handle anything life threw my way.

But then, a lifeline appeared—my rabbi, who refused to let me drown in my despair. Without waiting for me to ask, he arranged therapy for me through the Jewish Family Services, ensuring I received the help I desperately needed at no cost. For the first time, I was confronted with a kind of strength that had nothing to do with independence and everything to do with acceptance.

Initially, therapy felt like an admission of failure. I had always seen needing help as a sign of weakness, proof that I wasn't capable enough. But as the weeks turned into months, something extraordinary happened. The sessions became a sanctuary, a place where I could lay down the burdens I had been carrying alone for far too long. My therapist's office became a space where vulnerability was not just accepted but encouraged.

From a neuroscientific perspective, receiving help activates the ventral striatum, a region of the brain associated with reward and positive social interactions. Studies conducted at UCLA have shown that acts of giving and receiving support release oxytocin, a hormone that fosters trust and emotional bonding. This biological response not only enhances our mood but also strengthens our social connections, creating a positive feedback loop that promotes mental well-being.

Moreover, allowing ourselves to receive help reduces the cortisol levels associated with stress, aiding in physical recovery and mental resilience. This understanding reveals that receiving is not just a passive act but an active engagement in the cycle of human connection, fostering deeper relationships and emotional strength.

The experience in Texas taught me a lesson that no amount of success or self-reliance ever could—true strength lies not in enduring alone but in knowing when to accept a lifeline. It is a humbling realization that shifts our understanding of power, from one of control and dominance to one of trust and community.

Accepting help does not diminish us; it enriches us. It opens doors to new perspectives, fosters deeper connections, and cultivates a sense of belonging that solitary strength could never provide. When we allow ourselves to receive, we invite others into our journey, transforming our struggles into shared experiences and our victories into collective celebrations.

Ironically, learning to receive has made me a better giver. Understanding the courage it takes to accept help has deepened my empathy, allowing me to offer support in ways that are more meaningful and sincere. Receiving is not the end of strength; it is the beginning of a reciprocal cycle that empowers everyone involved.

In letting go of the need to be invulnerable, we discover a new kind of power—a power rooted in trust, humility, and the unbreakable bonds of human connection. This is the paradox of strength: that in our moments of greatest vulnerability, we find our true resilience.

Stepping into the Unknown with Trust

Life is inherently uncertain, and the more we try to control it, the more elusive control becomes. It's like grasping at the wind—no matter how tightly you try to hold on, it slips through your fingers. In the face of the unknown, we often panic, thinking that our lack of control will lead to failure. But in truth, it is our attachment to certainty that binds us, not the uncertainty itself. Stepping into the unknown is an act of faith—a faith not in some outside force but in our own ability to navigate uncertainty and grow through it.

Fear of the unknown is a fundamental aspect of human nature. Evolutionarily, it served us well to avoid potential dangers and threats in our environment, ensuring our survival. But today, many of the fears we experience are not life-threatening. Instead, they are rooted in our anxiety about outcomes we cannot predict—whether it's about a business venture, a personal relationship, or even a move to a new city. Yet, when we lean into uncertainty rather than avoid it, something remarkable happens.

A study conducted at Stanford University found that our brains have a tendency to overestimate the likelihood of negative outcomes in uncertain situations. The research showed that when faced with the unknown, our brains activate the amygdala, the part of the brain associated with fear and anxiety. However, when we confront this fear head-on—whether through mindfulness, exposure, or simply allowing ourselves to embrace uncertainty—we activate the prefrontal cortex, the part of the brain responsible for rational thinking, decision-making, and problem-solving. This shift in brain activity shows that when we stop avoiding uncertainty, we can harness our higher cognitive functions, giving us the clarity and strength to move forward with confidence.

The decision to let go of control is one that takes deep courage. But true surrender is not about passively allowing life to happen to us. It is about actively choosing to trust the process and release the need for certainty. This was something I had to learn the hard way during my entrepreneurial journey, when I decided to build my own businesses. With no roadmap and no guarantee of success, I was stepping into uncharted territory.

At first, I tried to control everything. I meticulously planned every step, worried over every decision, and tried to anticipate every challenge. But what I didn't realize was that my intense need for control was actually stifling my ability to see opportunities. I was so fixated on avoiding failure that I missed the lessons embedded in every setback. It wasn't until I started to let go of the need for control that my perspective shifted. Suddenly, I was able to embrace the uncertainty, adapt to changing circumstances, and move forward with an open mind.

From a neurological standpoint, trust is a critical component of navigating uncertainty. A study from the University of California, Berkeley, found that trust activates the dopaminergic system in the brain, which is responsible for feelings of reward and motivation. When we trust, our brain rewards us with positive emotions and a sense of fulfillment, even in the absence of certainty. This is why letting go of the need to control can actually make us feel more empowered—not less.

Additionally, when we trust in the process and embrace uncertainty, we activate the brain's hippocampus, which is responsible for memory and learning. By stepping into the unknown, we allow our brains to reorganize and adapt, promoting neuroplasticity—the brain's ability to form new connections and change in response to experience. This means that every time we face uncertainty and choose to trust, we are literally rewiring our brain to become more resilient and adaptable to future challenges.

Faith, in this context, doesn't have to be religious. It can simply be the belief that no matter what happens, we will be okay. It's the trust that life has a way of unfolding as it should, even if it's not in the way we expected. This kind of faith is rooted in the understanding that life is a dynamic process, constantly shifting and evolving. We are not in control of every outcome, but we are always in control of how we respond to what comes our way.

Faith in the unknown is liberating because it removes the pressure of needing to have everything figured out. It allows us to let go of the constant need to control every detail, and instead, move forward with confidence that whatever happens will serve us in some way. There's a certain peace that comes with this type of trust, one that comes not from certainty but from a deep sense of inner knowing that we can handle whatever life presents.

The transformative power of surrender lies in its ability to shift our relationship with the unknown. Instead of fearing it, we learn to embrace it as a space of possibility and growth. By surrendering to uncertainty, we unlock new levels of creativity, resilience, and adaptability. We stop fearing what could go wrong and start trusting that whatever unfolds is an opportunity to evolve.

In the process, we also create space for new opportunities to come into our lives. When we stop trying to control the outcome, we open ourselves up to receiving what we truly need. The universe, or whatever force we believe in, has a way of guiding us toward what is right for us, but only if we are willing to trust in the process and surrender our attachment to specific outcomes.

I have witnessed the power of surrender firsthand in the lives of people I admire. One such example is a mentor of mine, who, after decades of running a successful business, was faced with the unexpected collapse of his company. At first, he fought against the situation, trying everything he could to salvage what was left. But when he finally surrendered and let go of his need to fix everything, new opportunities began to unfold. He was offered a position at a global organization that aligned perfectly with his skills, but one that he would never have considered had he remained attached to his previous business.

In his case, surrender didn't mean giving up. It meant letting go of his identity as the owner of a company and allowing himself to step into a new role that offered greater fulfillment. It was only when he relinquished control that the doors of opportunity opened for him, leading him to a place where he felt more aligned with his true purpose.

Stepping into the unknown is an act of profound trust, both in ourselves and in life itself. It requires the courage to let go of the need to control, to embrace uncertainty, and to trust that everything will unfold as it is meant to. When we surrender, we open ourselves up to new possibilities and opportunities that we could never have predicted. It is through this act of faith, of letting go, that we discover not only new paths but also a deeper sense of peace and fulfillment.

In the end, the true beauty of surrender is not in what we relinquish, but in what we gain. By stepping into the unknown with trust, we are not walking away from control; we are stepping into a higher form of control—one that comes from trust, adaptability, and a deep connection to the flow of life.

Learning to Receive

We are taught from an early age that strength means self-sufficiency. Independence is championed as a virtue, while needing help is often seen as weakness. This conditioning seeps into our subconscious, shaping how we interact with the world. We become people who offer but do not ask, who give but do not receive. We pride ourselves on being the strong ones—the ones who carry the burdens, who solve problems, who never need to lean on anyone else.

But what happens when life brings us to a place where we cannot stand on our own? What happens when we are forced to confront the uncomfortable truth that we do need help?

For me, one of the most humbling experiences of my life came when I had no choice but to receive. In Texas, after a series of financial losses, career pivots, and personal upheavals, I found myself at a breaking point. I was no longer the provider, the problem-solver, the one in control. I had always been someone who others relied on, but suddenly,

I was the one in need. And yet, I resisted every offer of help.

Even as my rabbi arranged for me to receive therapy at the Jewish Family Services, I felt a deep discomfort. My instinct was to reject it. Accepting help felt like admitting defeat. I told myself I should be able to handle it alone, that taking something for free meant I had failed. I carried so much shame about needing support that I almost let it drown me.

Studies in psychology reveal that many people struggle to accept help, even when they desperately need it. Research by Kayla Good, a social psychologist at the University of Pittsburgh, found that people often refuse assistance because they fear it will make them appear incompetent or indebted to others. This phenomenon, known as the "burden paradox," shows that we are more comfortable offering help than receiving it because we believe it preserves our autonomy and self-worth.

However, neuroscientific research tells a different story. When we allow ourselves to receive, our brains activate the same neural pathways associated with giving. In other words, just as generosity strengthens human connection, so does the act of accepting generosity. The simple act of receiving fosters trust, deepens relationships, and reinforces social bonds.

In my own journey, I eventually realized that my reluctance to receive help was not about pride—it was about fear. Fear that if I stopped being the strong one, people would see me differently. Fear that accepting help would mean losing control of my own narrative.

But in truth, receiving is one of the most powerful acts of surrender.

What I once saw as weakness, I came to understand as strength. It takes courage to say, "I can't do this alone." It takes humility to allow others to show up for us. And when we let them, something beautiful happens—we experience the depth of human connection in a way we never could while standing alone.

That therapy in Texas? It changed everything. It gave me clarity when my thoughts were clouded. It allowed me to break patterns of self-isolation that had kept me trapped in my own suffering. More than anything, it taught me that real strength isn't about carrying the weight of the world alone—it's about knowing when to let someone help you carry it.

This experience fundamentally changed how I view giving and receiving. I used to believe that offering help was the highest form of generosity. But I now know that allowing others to help us is equally, if not more, profound.

Think about it—have you ever offered to help someone, only to be rejected? It feels like an emotional block, a missed opportunity to connect. When we refuse help, we don't just deprive ourselves of support—we deprive others of the chance to show love, care, and generosity.

In Judaism, the concept of tzedakah (charitable giving) teaches that giving is not just an act of kindness, but a moral responsibility. However, the highest form of tzedakah is helping someone in a way that preserves their dignity—by creating opportunities for them rather than making them feel dependent. This means that both giving and receiving must come from a place of trust, openness, and surrender.

When I finally allowed myself to receive, I saw what I had been blind to for so long: I was not alone, and I never had been.

Once I learned to receive, I noticed that something unexpected happened—I became better at giving. Because I had been on the other side, because I knew what it felt like to struggle with the idea of asking for help, I became more attuned to the quiet suffering of others.

I began to see the moments when people, like me, wanted to ask but were too afraid. I started offering help in a way that made people feel empowered rather than ashamed. Receiving had taught me how to give more meaningfully.

We often associate surrender with loss, but sometimes surrender is simply saying yes—to love, to support, to connection. We do not have to walk through life proving our strength by isolation. We do not have to suffer alone.

The walls we build around ourselves—walls of pride, of fear, of self-reliance—do not make us stronger. They make us lonelier. And the moment we allow those walls to come down, we discover something extraordinary: people are waiting on the other side, ready to meet us with open hands.

Receiving does not diminish us. It completes us.

When we learn to receive, we stop treating life as a battle we must fight alone. We begin to understand that true strength is found in connection, in trust, and in the courage to open our hearts to others.

The Courage to Walk Into Uncertainty

We are taught to plan, to prepare, to make decisions based on security and predictability. From an early age, we are conditioned to believe that stability is the goal—that certainty is the foundation upon which a successful life is built. But life, in its rawest form, is uncertain. And the greatest leaps we take, the moments that define and transform us, often require stepping into the unknown.

There have been many moments in my life when I had to take a leap of faith, but one that stands out was my decision to build my own businesses rather than follow a conventional career path. It was a decision that defied logic in many ways. There was no guarantee of success, no safety net, no clear roadmap to follow. I was walking into uncertainty, relying only on instinct, resilience, and trust in my ability to adapt.

Psychologists have long studied the relationship between uncertainty and personal growth. Research published in the Journal of Personality and Social Psychology suggests that humans have a fundamental aversion to uncertainty because it triggers our survival instincts. The brain perceives the unknown as a potential threat, activating the amygdala—the same region responsible for fear responses. This is why uncertainty can feel so deeply unsettling, even when no immediate danger exists.

However, neuroscientific research also tells us that uncertainty is a powerful catalyst for growth. Studies show that when we step outside of our comfort zones, the brain releases dopamine, the neurotransmitter associated with learning and motivation. This means that while uncertainty may feel like a threat, it is also the key to unlocking creativity, problem-solving, and resilience.

In other words, stepping into the unknown isn't just an emotional challenge—it is a neurological gateway to transformation.

The first time I truly grasped the weight of uncertainty, I was standing at a crossroads in my life. I had already walked away from the stability of a corporate job. I had already invested months into my entrepreneurial pursuits. But I reached a moment when everything was on the line— financially, emotionally, and professionally. I had built something from the ground up, and yet, there were no guarantees.

I remember sitting alone in a rented office space in Abu Dhabi, staring at a whiteboard filled with projections and strategies. But no amount of planning could give me certainty. No formula could tell me if I would succeed. And in that moment, I had a choice: retreat into the familiar, or lean fully into the unknown.

It was terrifying. Every instinct in my body screamed at me to find an escape route, to look for something safer. But deep down, I knew that safety wasn't what I was searching for—growth was. And growth required trust.

There is a misconception that surrender means passivity—that stepping into uncertainty is about giving up control entirely. But true surrender is not about standing still; it is about moving forward without needing to control the outcome. It is the difference between fearfully hesitating at the edge of a cliff and diving in, trusting that the water below will carry you.

Spiritual traditions around the world emphasize this idea. In Buddhism, the concept of anicca—impermanence—teaches that everything in life is constantly changing, and our suffering comes from resisting that change. In Jewish mysticism, emunah, or deep faith, is the belief that even in the absence of clarity, there is a path unfolding beneath our feet.

The greatest breakthroughs happen when we release the need for certainty and embrace the unknown with open hands.

Looking back, I see that every major turning point in my life came from a moment of surrender. Not surrender in the sense of giving up, but surrender in the sense of allowing life to unfold without forcing it.

I had to surrender to the unknown when I left a stable career to pursue something I believed in.

I had to surrender to the unknown when I lost everything and had to start over.

I had to surrender to the unknown when relationships ended, when plans fell apart, when the life I thought I was building turned into something completely different.

Every single time, uncertainty felt like a cliff's edge. But every single time, stepping forward led to something greater than I could have imagined.

That is the paradox of uncertainty—it feels like a loss of control, but in reality, it is an invitation to something bigger than ourselves.

At its core, walking into uncertainty is about trusting ourselves and the process of life. It is about recognizing that control is an illusion, and that what we fear the most—stepping into the unknown—is often the very thing that will set us free.

Many people spend their lives waiting for the right moment, the perfect plan, the guarantee of success. But life does not give us guarantees—it gives us opportunities. And the people who truly thrive are not those who avoid uncertainty, but those who embrace it, who dance with it, who see it not as a threat, but as a doorway.

If there is something you have been afraid to do, if there is a path you have been hesitating to take because the outcome is unclear, I invite you to consider this:

What if the uncertainty is not a reason to stop, but a sign that you are exactly where you need to be?

Because the truth is, no one ever steps into greatness without stepping into the unknown first.

And the greatest journeys are never the ones with the clearest maps. They are the ones where we trust the road will reveal itself as we walk.

Chapter 7: The Art of Allowing

The Illusion of Control: Why We Struggle to Let Life Unfold

We are taught from a young age that hard work, careful planning, and relentless effort will lead us exactly where we want to go. Society glorifies control as the key to success—whether it's controlling our schedules, finances, relationships, or even the way we are perceived. The idea that we must make things happen has been drilled into us, turning surrender into something that feels unnatural, even irresponsible.

But what if this is a flawed way of thinking? What if our constant striving, our endless attempts to force life into our preferred shape, are actually working against us?

Research in psychology and neuroscience reveals a deep human attachment to control. The illusion of control bias, a term first coined by psychologist Ellen Langer in 1975, describes our tendency to overestimate our ability to influence outcomes—even in situations where chance plays the dominant role. Studies have shown that people feel more confident in their ability to predict the stock market, win at gambling, or even influence personal relationships simply because they are actively engaged, when in reality, many factors remain beyond their influence.

A well-known experiment in behavioral psychology illustrates this phenomenon. In a study by Alloy and Abramson, participants were asked to press a button to turn on a light. However, the button had no real control over when the light turned on; it was pre-programmed to illuminate randomly. Nonetheless, participants overwhelmingly believed that their actions had a direct effect on the outcome. This experiment demonstrated just how deeply ingrained the illusion of control is—our minds naturally seek patterns and causality, even when none exist.

This illusion is comforting because it gives us a sense of security in an unpredictable world. But paradoxically, the more we try to force control, the more anxiety and distress we create. A 2021 study published in the Journal of Anxiety Disorders found that individuals with high levels of control-seeking behavior tend to have increased rates of anxiety, depression, and emotional exhaustion. The reason? When we operate under the assumption that we can and should be in control, any deviation from our expectations feels like failure. The unpredictability of life becomes a threat, rather than an opportunity.

The irony is that while control makes us feel safer, studies show that people who embrace uncertainty and allow life to unfold naturally report greater well-being and life satisfaction. A 2017 study published in Psychological Science found that individuals who practiced psychological flexibility—the ability to adapt to change, accept discomfort, and remain open to unexpected outcomes—had lower stress levels and greater resilience.

Moreover, neuroscience confirms that letting go can rewire our brains for peace and creativity. When we are fixated on controlling everything, we engage the dorsolateral prefrontal cortex, the part of the brain responsible for planning, problem-solving, and rigid thinking. However, when we practice acceptance and allowing, we activate the default mode network (DMN)—a neural system linked to creativity, insight, and higher consciousness. This shift explains why breakthroughs often happen when we stop forcing them— why solutions appear in the shower, on a walk, or in a moment of stillness rather than in the grip of relentless effort.

Beyond the cognitive and neurological effects, the emotional toll of control-seeking behavior is profound. When we expect life to follow our script and it doesn't, we experience anger, frustration, guilt, and shame. This is particularly evident in high-achievers and perfectionists, who frequently report feeling burned out, unfulfilled, and disconnected from themselves despite their outward success.

A 2020 report by the American Psychological Association (APA) found that burnout rates among professionals have skyrocketed due to an increasing emphasis on hyper-productivity and personal control. The more people try to micromanage their lives, the more they feel trapped in cycles of stress, self-doubt, and dissatisfaction.

This cycle is what keeps us from surrendering. We believe that if we can just try harder, be more disciplined, or make the perfect decision, we will finally feel in control. But the truth is that peace doesn't come from control—it comes from trust.

Letting Life Come to You

Early in 2013, I had just finished developing a script that told a compelling story set in the Middle East. As part of my approach to packaging projects organically, I set out to find a director who could bring the authenticity, depth, and vision the story deserved. My search led me to a rising filmmaker from Egypt. His body of work resonated with me instantly—his storytelling, his cinematic style, his understanding of the cultural nuances that were integral to my film. I felt strongly that he was the right match, the creative partner who could elevate this project beyond what I had imagined.

Fueled by certainty, I began the process of reaching out to him. I sent emails, leveraged mutual connections, and tried every possible avenue to establish contact. I was persistent, confident that my effort and determination would eventually yield results. But no matter what I did, he never responded. I reached out through industry contacts, through friends of friends, through the film community in Cairo—yet every attempt was met with silence. Weeks turned into months. Frustration crept in, and what had started as enthusiasm turned into a battle against the very idea that something this important could remain beyond my reach.

Eventually, I reached a point of surrender. I let it go—not out of resignation, but because it became clear that my relentless pursuit was not yielding the results I expected. Maybe it wasn't meant to be. Maybe I needed to step back and trust the process.

Then, something remarkable happened.

One afternoon, while having lunch with a friend in Dubai, the topic of my film project came up in conversation. It was a casual discussion, with no particular agenda. I simply shared the idea, the passion I had for the story, and mentioned my unsuccessful attempts to connect with my chosen director. My friend listened, nodded, and the conversation moved on. It felt like nothing more than a passing remark.

The very next day, that same friend called me—with the director in question on the phone.

Within weeks, everything shifted. What once felt like an insurmountable dead end transformed into an open door. Not only did I finally connect with the director, but through a series of unexpected developments, we ended up cofounding a production company together in Abu Dhabi. The outcome was bigger than I had originally envisioned—not just a collaboration, but a partnership that shaped the next chapter of my career.

At first glance, it would be easy to dismiss this as luck or coincidence. But psychological and behavioral research suggests that this phenomenon—when opportunities seem to "appear" once we stop forcing them—has scientific roots.

Studies on serendipity and non-linear success reveal that many of life's greatest breakthroughs come not from direct effort, but from what researchers call peripheral awareness—the ability to stay open to unexpected opportunities rather than fixating on rigid plans. In other words, our best opportunities often come not from the doors we push open, but from the ones that open naturally when we stop forcing them.

Psychologist Ellen Langer introduced the concept of the illusion of control, which explains why we often believe that our sheer persistence dictates success. While effort and determination are undeniably important, cognitive science suggests that over-managing an outcome can actually create more resistance, blocking spontaneous solutions from emerging.

This is because the brain operates in two distinct processing modes:

1. Focused Attention Mode – When we fixate on a single outcome, we narrow our mental framework, often overlooking alternative paths that may be more aligned with our goals.

2. Diffuse Awareness Mode – When we relax our mental grip, our brain shifts into a state that allows insight, intuition, and unexpected connections to surface. This is why breakthroughs often happen not when we force solutions, but when we step away—during walks, in the shower, or in casual conversations.

In my case, letting go of the obsessive pursuit of a specific outcome created space for a natural connection to unfold. My conversation in Dubai wasn't engineered—it was organic, effortless. And that's precisely why it worked.

The belief that we can control every aspect of our lives is one of the greatest illusions we hold. We live in a world that glorifies hustle culture, telling us that if we just push hard enough, knock on enough doors, and refuse to take no for an answer, we will eventually "make it." While persistence is a powerful force, it is not the only force at play.

When we focus too narrowly on a single path, we blind ourselves to the alternatives that might be even better.

In the case of my film project, had I continued chasing the director with increasing intensity, it's unlikely I would have connected with him in the way I eventually did. Had I resisted surrendering, I might have missed the conversation in Dubai altogether. Letting go didn't mean giving up—it meant creating space for alignment.

Surrender is not passivity. It is trust. It is the understanding that while effort is necessary, so is openness. The opportunities that are meant for us often arrive in ways we could have never predicted.

Letting life come to you is not about doing nothing. This doesn't mean we sit back and wait for life to hand us what we want. It means we take action, but then allow space for the unexpected to unfold.

We pursue our goals, but we also allow for course corrections.

We ask for what we want, but we remain receptive to answers that come in unexpected ways.

We trust that when something doesn't happen on our timeline, it doesn't mean it will never happen—it means there is a better way for it to unfold.

This principle applies to everything—from career breakthroughs to relationships to personal growth.

If something is meant for us, we don't have to exhaust ourselves chasing it. We only need to be in the right place, in the right state of openness, when it arrives.

Trusting in Divine Timing

There are moments in life when we are certain that things should unfold in a particular way. We plan, prepare, and pour every ounce of energy into securing the outcomes we believe we deserve. Yet, despite our best efforts, life does not always comply. In those moments, it is easy to feel abandoned—by people, by circumstances, even by God.

I know this feeling intimately.

There was a period in my life when everything I had built, everything I had trusted in, crumbled in an instant. Financially, I had suffered staggering losses. But it wasn't just the money—it was the security, the identity, the carefully structured future I had mapped out with precision. It was the loss of certainty. The loss of faith.

For months, I wrestled with questions that had no immediate answers. Had I made the wrong choices? Was I being punished? Had I failed myself and those who had put their trust in me? I searched for explanations, trying to force meaning into a situation that felt meaningless. But no matter how much I analyzed, I found no resolution—only deeper frustration.

Psychologists have long studied the human need for control, and research suggests that our brains are wired to resist uncertainty. Studies show that the anterior cingulate cortex, the part of the brain responsible for detecting threats, is highly sensitive to unpredictability. When we don't know what's coming next, our stress response is triggered, leading to heightened anxiety and even physical distress.

This need for control makes it difficult to trust in timing beyond our own. We want results now. We want clarity now. We want answers now. But life is not built around our timelines—it moves according to its own rhythm.

Kabbalistic teachings refer to this as Seder HaHishtalshelut—the divine order of unfolding. According to this philosophy, everything in the universe is structured within a spiritual hierarchy, cascading from the infinite into the finite, from the unseen to the seen. Nothing is random. Nothing is out of place. Even what seems like chaos is part of a greater, structured design.

At the time of my greatest losses, I struggled to see that. But as I stood amidst the rubble of what once was, I began to understand that what I had perceived as destruction was actually a clearing. A necessary emptying to make space for something greater.

The reason we resist divine timing is simple: we mistake waiting for stagnation.

We assume that if something isn't happening when we want it to, it won't happen at all.

We believe that stillness means failure.

We equate delay with rejection.

But in reality, delay is often redirection.

Neuroscientists studying the Default Mode Network (DMN)—the brain's system responsible for introspection and long-term planning—have found that moments of waiting and uncertainty actually enhance cognitive processing and creative insight. In other words, when we are forced to pause, our brains reorganize information, allowing us to see solutions and opportunities that were previously invisible.

What if the very thing we are fighting against—waiting—is the thing that will lead us to the answer?

One of the most profound ideas in Jewish mysticism is the concept of Ohr HaGanuz—the Hidden Light. The Baal Shem Tov, the founder of Hasidic Judaism, taught that delays and hardships conceal divine wisdom that is not yet ready to be revealed. If we were given everything we wanted, exactly when we wanted it, we would be unprepared to handle it.

The Zohar, one of the foundational texts of Kabbalah, explains:

"There are blessings that come as open gifts, and there are blessings that come concealed—hidden in the form of challenges, delays, and even losses. The wise do not curse the darkness, for they know it is only the wrapping of a greater light."

This teaching transformed my perspective. Instead of seeing my financial losses as punishment or misfortune, I began to ask:

What is this experience trying to teach me?

What space is being created by what I have lost?

What if this is not an end, but a beginning?

As I let go of my need to force things into place, something shifted. I started making decisions not from desperation, but from alignment. I no longer felt the urgency to cling to what was. I became open to what could be.

And then, something even more surprising happened: the right opportunities started arriving on their own.

A new business venture—one that was more aligned with my values—emerged. A book deal—something I hadn't even planned for—materialized. New relationships—ones that were healthier and more expansive—began forming.

It was then that I truly understood: when we release our attachment to timing, life moves more fluidly.

The job that didn't happen, the relationship that ended, the investment that fell through—all of it was not rejection, but protection.

The things I had desperately clung to were things that needed to fall away so that my life could expand in ways I could never have orchestrated on my own.

Letting go of control does not mean sitting idly by, waiting for life to happen. It means acting with intention but surrendering the outcome.

We take steps forward, but we do not rush.

We make plans, but we remain open to better ones.

We trust that what is meant for us will arrive—not a moment too late, nor a moment too soon.

True trust is not found in forcing. It is found in allowing.

Looking back, I now see that what I once feared as loss was actually the divine making space for something greater. The greatest moments—the ones that define us—rarely arrive according to our schedules.

The job we didn't get leads us to the career we were truly meant for.

The relationship that ended clears the path for one that nourishes our soul.

The door that closed redirects us to one that we never would have knocked on otherwise.

We are not abandoned. We are not being punished. We are being prepared.

The universe moves in perfect timing.

Our only task is to trust it.

Releasing the Need for Immediate Clarity

For much of my life, I had been conditioned to believe that clarity was something to be pursued relentlessly, that answers must be wrestled into submission through logic, planning, and sheer force of will. The unknown was something to be conquered, not trusted. Ambiguity felt like a problem to be solved, not an experience to be lived.

But then, in a single act of surrender, I let go of that need—and everything changed.

I still remember the moment. After attending my first meditation retreat in Los Angeles, I walked away feeling lighter than I had in years. But it wasn't because I had figured everything out. In fact, quite the opposite—I had no concrete plan, no certainty about what was coming next. But, for the first time, that didn't feel like failure—it felt like freedom.

It wasn't the kind of clarity that came from knowing exactly what to do next. It was a deeper kind of clarity—the kind that whispers, "You don't have to know yet."

For so long, I had believed that my security depended on having a roadmap—that the only way forward was through meticulous planning and ironclad certainty. But in that retreat, I encountered something radically different.

In stillness, I realized that the need for clarity is an illusion. Life does not unfold in linear, pre-scripted steps. Trying to force the unknown into a framework of control is like trying to bottle the ocean—it only creates frustration, rigidity, and resistance.

Neuroscience supports this idea. Research by Mihaly Csikszentmihalyi, the renowned psychologist behind the concept of flow state, reveals that people perform at their best not when they are overanalyzing, but when they are immersed in the present moment. The paradox of clarity is that it often arrives not when we force it, but when we release the need for it.

Another study by John Kounios and Mark Beeman found that the brain's default mode network (DMN)—the system responsible for subconscious processing—activates during moments of rest, leading to sudden bursts of insight. This suggests that certainty and clarity emerge naturally when we stop overthinking and allow space for creativity and wisdom to surface.

I didn't fully understand this yet when I left Texas. All I knew was that something inside me told me to go.

Without a solid plan or even a stable home base, I packed my things and moved to Los Angeles. Friends and colleagues thought I was making an impulsive decision.

"What's the plan?" they asked.

I didn't have one. But for the first time, I didn't need one.

What happened next was nothing short of remarkable. Everything I had been struggling to piece together in Texas began to flow effortlessly in LA.

Meetings that once took months to arrange happened organically over coffee.

Opportunities presented themselves without endless strategizing.

The right people seemed to show up at just the right time.

It was as if life had been waiting for me to stop fighting for control so it could guide me where I needed to be. By loosening my grip, I opened my hands to receive.

This aligns with Kabbalistic philosophy, particularly the concept of Hashgacha Pratit (Divine Providence). Jewish mysticism teaches that events unfold according to a larger, unseen order—one that is impossible to fully grasp in the moment. The Baal Shem Tov taught that what appears to be randomness is actually divine orchestration, and our role is not to micromanage, but to be aware.

This is not passivity—it is attunement.

Kabbalah calls this state "bitachon"—a deep, unshakable trust in the unfolding of life. It is not resignation, but an active surrender—one that allows synchronicity, guidance, and unexpected solutions to emerge.

Western psychology echoes this wisdom. Cognitive science has shown that excessive cognitive effort—especially in trying to force solutions—can actually inhibit creative insight.

Neuroscientist Arne Dietrich found that during moments of forced problem-solving, the prefrontal cortex (the brain's command center for logical reasoning) overrides intuitive processing, making it harder to generate creative solutions.

Schooler et al. discovered that people are more likely to have "aha" moments when they engage in effortless activities—walking, showering, even daydreaming—rather than when they actively try to solve problems.

This research suggests that letting go of the desperate grasp for clarity does not lead to chaos—it leads to breakthroughs.

I've since come to believe that clarity is a byproduct of surrender.

The need to know what's coming next is an illusion born from fear.

The demand for certainty closes us off to unseen opportunities.

The best decisions I have ever made—the ones that shaped my career, deepened my relationships, and led me to profound spiritual insights—were not the ones I planned meticulously.

They were the ones I stepped into with open hands, trusting that the path would reveal itself.

And it always did.

The Power of Openness

There was a night during the 2016 Cannes Film Festival when I was completely drained. After back-to-back meetings, screenings, and networking events, the last thing I wanted to do was attend yet another after-party. I had no energy left, and if I'm being honest, I was beginning to question the purpose of it all. Did any of these events truly make a difference? Was I just exhausting myself for the illusion of productivity?

I had already mapped out my plans for the festival meticulously. I had identified key decision-makers, set up meetings, and attended the right panels. And yet, at the end of the day, the breakthroughs I had anticipated hadn't materialized. That night, I was tempted to retreat to my hotel room and call it a day.

But at the last moment, I gave in to the pressure. I told myself, Just show up. See what happens.

That night, I met a Danish film producer—a woman I might never have encountered under different circumstances. Our conversation started casually, touching on cinema, storytelling, and the evolving landscape of streaming platforms. At first, it was nothing extraordinary—just another industry conversation. But as the night unfolded, what began as small talk turned into something far more significant.

She was looking for fresh ideas.

I had projects that aligned with her vision.

A simple, unplanned conversation turned into a two-year collaboration developing two TV shows—an opportunity that would never have happened had I followed my initial instinct to say no.

This wasn't an isolated incident. Time and time again, I've seen how stepping into situations I initially resisted led to opportunities I never could have planned for.

Neuroscientists have found that openness to experience is one of the strongest predictors of creativity, success, and personal growth. In psychological research, the Big Five personality model highlights "openness" as the trait most associated with curiosity, adaptability, and the ability to recognize unexpected opportunities.

Studies on cognitive flexibility suggest that individuals who embrace uncertainty and remain open to new experiences tend to recognize more opportunities than those who rigidly adhere to a set plan. When we surrender our need for complete control, we activate parts of the brain responsible for creativity, problem-solving, and innovation.

The Default Mode Network (DMN)—a system in the brain responsible for creativity, intuition, and insight—is more active when we are open to new experiences.

Psychologists speak of counterfactual thinking, the "what if" scenarios that shape our choices. Research suggests that people who reflect on moments when an unexpected turn led to something positive are more likely to embrace uncertainty rather than fear it. In other words, openness doesn't just create new possibilities; it actually reprograms the brain to expect them.

This aligns perfectly with the way openness creates momentum. When we are locked into rigid expectations, we tend to reject opportunities that don't match our preconceived ideas of success. But when we show up without resistance, we become magnets for serendipity.

This idea is beautifully reflected in Kabbalistic teachings, particularly the concept of Tzimtzum. In Jewish mysticism, Tzimtzum refers to the divine act of contraction—God making space for the world to exist. The lesson is profound:

In order for something new to emerge, we must create space for it.

This applies to personal growth, relationships, and professional success. The tighter we cling to a single, fixed outcome, the less room we leave for life to surprise us.

This mirrors the principle of receptivity—that true transformation happens when we stop resisting and start receiving. By showing up with curiosity rather than rigid expectations, we align ourselves with opportunities we might never have consciously pursued.

The Zohar, a foundational text of Kabbalah, teaches:

"The vessel that receives the most light is the one that is empty, open, and ready."

Openness is not about passivity. It is about alignment.

Looking back, I could have easily skipped that Cannes party. I could have followed my exhaustion, chosen comfort, and convinced myself that nothing important would come from one more conversation.

And yet, choosing to remain open allowed something entirely unexpected to unfold.

That moment taught me a lesson I've carried ever since: The greatest opportunities, partnerships, and personal breakthroughs don't come from meticulously controlled plans. They emerge from spontaneous moments of saying "yes" when we could have said "no."

Openness isn't about waiting for life to happen to us.

It's about stepping forward, even when we don't see the full picture.

It's about trusting that what we need will find us—often in ways we never anticipated.

And that's the power of letting go of control and allowing life to flow through us.

Saying Yes to Life

After the 2008 financial crisis, I found myself at a cross-roads. Everything I had meticulously planned—every strategy, every investment, every calculated move—was suddenly at a risk of collapse overnight. For years, I had measured success through stability, control, and long-term planning. And yet, in the span of a few months, all of that became irrelevant.

At first, I resisted. I kept looking for ways to regain my footing, trying to reconstruct the life I had envisioned. But nothing worked. The world had changed, and I was fighting against a tide that no longer existed. That's when I made a decision that would alter the course of my life completely.

I abandoned the idea of rigid planning and embraced a more intuitive, spontaneous approach to life. Instead of forcing things to happen, I allowed life to unfold. That decision led me to Beirut, where I started writing what would become a bestselling sci-fi trilogy. It led me to unexpected opportunities—getting published, lecturing at a university, and forming connections that shaped the next decade of my career.

None of it was part of my plan. But all of it became far more meaningful than anything I had tried to control before.

There's a psychological phenomenon called openness to experience, one of the five major personality traits in psychology. Research shows that people who embrace spontaneity and uncertainty tend to be happier, more adaptable, and more resilient.

This aligns with positive psychology, which suggests that saying "yes" to life increases our ability to experience flow states—moments of deep immersion where creativity and intuition flourish . People who take more risks, explore new opportunities, and step outside their comfort zones activate neural pathways associated with dopamine release, the neurotransmitter responsible for motivation and pleasure.

Kabbalistic wisdom speaks of Ein Sof—the infinite, boundless energy of creation. To be in alignment with Ein Sof means to be in a state of continuous expansion, allowing life to shape us rather than clinging to a fixed identity. In this perspective, resistance blocks divine flow, while surrendering opens us to limitless possibilities.

The idea of bitachon (trust) in Jewish mysticism teaches that true faith is not just believing in a higher power but trusting the unfolding of events, even when they seem uncertain. When we say yes to life, we acknowledge that we are part of something bigger—something that is always guiding us toward growth.

Looking back, my greatest turning points didn't come from perfectly executed plans—they came from moments where I chose to let go and say yes.

Yes to uncertainty.

Yes to new experiences.

Yes to opportunities that didn't fit the blueprint I once thought was essential.

The world teaches us to control, to strategize, to protect ourselves from risk. But true fulfillment comes from allowing life to surprise us.

And when we do?

We step into something greater than we ever imagined.

Chapter 8: The Strength in Softness

For most of my life, I held onto a belief that felt as solid as the ground beneath my feet: money was the answer to security. It wasn't a theory I had questioned—it was a fact. It was something I saw, something I internalized through years of watching the world operate. Money was control. Money was safety. And safety meant freedom from fear.

This belief wasn't born in a vacuum. It was shaped by experience. Growing up, I watched people I admired chase financial stability as if their very existence depended on it. I saw the doors that opened for those with wealth and the silent, insidious constraints that choked those without it. I saw how money could turn a crisis into an inconvenience, how it could shield a person from the kind of humiliation and powerlessness that came with needing help. The message was clear: if you want to be untouchable, you must have enough to never need anyone.

And so, I chased.

I built. I accumulated. I invested. I moved from one opportunity to the next, structuring my entire life around the idea that as long as I kept climbing, I would never have to fall. And for a long time, this illusion worked. The numbers in my accounts confirmed my efforts. The status, the recognition, the invitations to exclusive circles—all of it reassured me that I was on the right track. Success was proof of security. And yet, beneath it all, something remained unresolved, something I refused to acknowledge:

I was still afraid.

Even with everything I had acquired, I was never fully at peace. The fear of losing it all, the fear of slipping, the fear of suddenly being unprotected—these anxieties lived beneath the surface, quiet but constant. The more I gained, the harder I gripped onto it, because deep down, I knew that my security was conditional. It wasn't rooted in anything intrinsic. It was tied to numbers, investments, business deals—things that could disappear overnight. But I ignored that reality. I thought if I just built more, stacked more, planned better—I could outrun that fear.

I couldn't.

Then came the collapse. A series of financial disasters wiped out everything I had built. It wasn't just a setback—it was a total dismantling of the fortress I had spent years constructing. The very thing I believed would protect me was gone.

And with it, my sense of self unraveled. Who was I without the success? Without the security I had built? If money was the answer, then what did it mean when I had nothing left?

I fought against the truth with everything in me. I strategized, I calculated, I searched for ways to rebuild as quickly as possible. But nothing worked. There was no immediate fix. And in that space—where all my efforts, all my plans, all my hard-earned wisdom failed—I came face to face with the one thing I had spent my life avoiding:

I wasn't in control.

For the first time, I had to sit with the discomfort of that truth. I had to acknowledge that security had never come from my bank account. It had never come from my achievements. It had always been an illusion.

I wasn't alone in this. Research in behavioral economics and psychology has shown that humans have an inherent tendency to seek control over their environment. The "illusion of control," a concept first introduced by psychologist Ellen Langer , describes how we overestimate our ability to influence events that are actually beyond our control. This cognitive bias is particularly strong in financial decision-making—studies have shown that people feel more secure when they believe their financial status is a result of their own actions, even when external factors (market fluctuations, economic downturns) play a far greater role than they acknowledge.

Furthermore, neuroscientists have found that the brain's fear response is closely linked to loss aversion—we experience the pain of losing money twice as intensely as we experience the pleasure of gaining it. This means that even when we achieve financial success, our brains are wired to focus on the risk of losing it, making it nearly impossible to feel truly secure.

So what does this mean?

It means that my attachment to wealth as a form of safety was not just a personal flaw—it was a deeply ingrained human instinct. It was my brain's way of trying to create stability in an unpredictable world. But just because something feels true doesn't mean it is true. And the real test came when I lost everything.

For months after the financial collapse, I existed in a state of internal war. Part of me still clung to my old belief, desperately trying to fix everything, to rebuild, to get back to the "secure" place I had once been. But another part of me—the part that had been silenced for years—began whispering something different:

What if I didn't need to rebuild what I had?

What if security wasn't something I could acquire externally?

What if I was enough, even without money, success, or recognition?

I didn't accept those thoughts easily. They felt reckless, almost sacrilegious. But something inside me was shifting, something deeper than logic, something beyond what my past experiences had taught me.

It took two years of therapy, meditation, and spiritual exploration for me to finally grasp the lesson life had been trying to teach me all along:

Security is not about what you have. It's about what you trust.

I had spent my whole life trusting wealth to protect me. But true security—the kind that can't be erased by market crashes or business failures—comes from something internal. It comes from a sense of self that isn't tied to possessions or achievements. It comes from knowing that even if everything external is taken away, you are still whole.

This wasn't just philosophical—it was profoundly spiritual. In Kabbalah, there is a concept called "Ein Sof"—the infinite divine presence that exists beyond limitation. The essence of Ein Sof teaches that all external forms of security are fleeting, and the only true source of stability is the connection to something greater than the material world. The moment we recognize that we are already enough, that we are held by something beyond wealth, beyond status, beyond achievement—that is the moment we become truly free.

I had spent my life worshipping a false god—the god of financial certainty. And in losing everything, I was given the rarest of opportunities: to build a security that no one could ever take away from me again.

Letting go of the belief that money equaled security didn't happen overnight. It was a process. A painful, often humiliating process. But as I stepped deeper into the unknown, I found something I had never known before:

Peace.

Not the peace that comes from knowing everything will work out exactly as I planned. But the peace that comes from knowing I no longer needed everything to go my way in order to be okay.

I still value financial stability. I still make plans. But I no longer live under the illusion that my worth, my safety, or my identity is tied to the numbers in my bank account.

Real security isn't found in what you own. It's found in what you're willing to let go of.

That is the truth I learned. And it has given me a kind of freedom I never knew was possible.

Facing the Fear of the Unknown

For most of my life, I believed that strength meant self-sufficiency. That being prepared, being in control, and never needing help was the only way to ensure survival. Asking for help meant weakness; vulnerability meant exposure; uncertainty meant failure. But life, as it often does, had other plans.

At one of the lowest points in my life, I found myself in a position I never imagined—completely without financial stability, without direction, and without the illusion that I could manage it all on my own. For the first time, I wasn't just facing difficulty; I was standing on the edge of a reality I had always feared: the unknown.

For a long time, I resisted it. I still tried to present myself as strong, as someone who could handle things alone. I pretended. I told myself I would figure it out, that I just needed more time, that the right opportunity or solution would come if I just worked harder. But deep down, I was exhausted. And more than that, I was scared—not just of failing, but of being seen as someone who needed to be saved.

Neuroscientists have studied how uncertainty affects the brain, and the results explain why we fear it so deeply. The human brain is wired to seek patterns, to predict outcomes, to create a sense of control. When faced with the unknown, the brain activates the amygdala, the region responsible for processing fear and threat. This is why uncertainty often feels physically unbearable—it triggers the same fight-or-flight response as an actual physical danger.

Studies also show that prolonged uncertainty leads to increased levels of cortisol, the stress hormone, which can impair decision-making, cause emotional exhaustion, and even lead to physical health issues. In other words, the more we fight against the unknown, the more we drain ourselves mentally, emotionally, and physically.

But research also suggests that people who cultivate psychological flexibility—the ability to accept uncertainty and adapt—experience lower stress levels, greater resilience, and even higher overall life satisfaction.

Eventually, I reached a breaking point. I could no longer pretend I had it under control. I couldn't keep resisting what was happening. I had to face the truth: I needed help. And more than that, I needed to stop seeing help as a failure.

When my rabbi stepped in and arranged for me to receive therapy at Jewish Family Services—without me having to pay a dime—I initially felt humiliated. I wasn't just accepting help; I was admitting that I needed it. The feeling was foreign, almost painful. But as the weeks passed, something shifted.

I realized that the people helping me didn't see me as weak. They saw me as human. The only one judging me was myself. The shame I had attached to receiving help was my construct, not reality.

In Kabbalistic thought, the concept of Emunah (faith) is not just about believing in God—it's about trusting the process of life, even when we cannot see the full picture. The Baal Shem Tov taught that moments of uncertainty are not punishments; they are invitations to surrender. Not to give up, but to give over—to recognize that the universe is moving in ways we cannot yet comprehend, and that the unknown is often where transformation begins.

Eastern philosophies echo this wisdom. In Taoism, the principle of wu wei (effortless action) teaches that when we stop resisting, we align ourselves with the natural flow of life. Instead of trying to force clarity, we allow it to emerge.

This shift in perspective was profound for me. Instead of seeing the unknown as something to fear, I began to see it as something to trust. I started asking myself a different question—not How do I stop this from happening? but What if this is happening for me, not to me?

Looking back, I realize that facing the unknown wasn't about losing control; it was about redefining it. Control isn't about having all the answers—it's about trusting yourself enough to move forward, even when you don't.

I learned that courage isn't the absence of fear. Courage is feeling the fear and taking the next step anyway.

And sometimes, the greatest act of courage is not in holding on, but in letting go.

The Pain of Releasing Something You Loved

Letting go is often romanticized as an act of strength, I probably did that myself a few times in this book, but in reality, it is one of the most excruciating things we can experience—especially when what we are releasing is something we deeply love. It is one thing to let go of something that is clearly toxic, unhealthy, or holding us back. But what about when we have to walk away from something beautiful? Something that, under different circumstances, could have lasted?

This was the dilemma I faced at the end of my third year in Houston. I was in a committed relationship with a woman who, by every measure, was the kind of partner I had always hoped to find. She was intelligent, kind, and deeply rooted in her values. Our relationship felt like home—safe, warm, and filled with genuine love. But as the months went by, I couldn't shake an internal restlessness, an ever-growing certainty that Houston was not where I was meant to be.

It wasn't just about geography. It was about my sense of self, my purpose, my need for an environment that could challenge and inspire me creatively. I had always known that my best work, my deepest fulfillment, came from being in vibrant, fast-moving creative communities. And while Houston had provided stability, it did not offer the kind of artistic and entrepreneurial energy that I craved. The realization became unavoidable: I needed to leave.

The problem? She wasn't leaving. Houston was her home, the city where she had built her career, her friendships, and the life she had always envisioned for herself. She was paying off a mortgage, running her own clinic, and deeply embedded in a community that meant everything to her. Asking her to leave was out of the question. And yet, staying meant abandoning something inside of me that I could not silence.

For months, I tried to rationalize a compromise. Maybe I could stay longer, make it work, find creative fulfillment in smaller ways. Maybe the love we shared would be enough to override the deeper pull I felt toward the next stage of my life. But in my heart, I already knew the truth. Some sacrifices feel noble in the moment but grow into regrets over time.

It was like standing at a crossroads where both choices involved loss. Staying meant losing a part of myself. Leaving meant losing her.

The Psychology of Heartbreak and Attachment

Neurological research has shown that emotional attachment, particularly in romantic relationships, triggers the same brain regions associated with physical pain . The loss of a loved one—whether through separation, death, or even conscious uncoupling—activates the brain's pain matrix, leading to withdrawal symptoms similar to those experienced in substance addiction.

This is why heartbreak feels like a bodily experience, not just an emotional one. It's why we lose our appetite, struggle to sleep, and feel a kind of visceral aching in our chests. The nervous system interprets attachment loss as a threat to survival, dating back to evolutionary mechanisms designed to keep us bonded for safety and reproduction.

Understanding this didn't make my decision any easier, but it did help me make sense of the deep sense of internal resistance I felt. We are wired to hold on. Letting go is not something the brain does willingly—it is something we must consciously teach it to accept.

Leaving felt like throwing my favorite story into the fire—watching the pages burn, knowing that no matter how much I cherished the words, I couldn't keep them. There was nothing wrong with our relationship. It wasn't broken. It wasn't toxic. It wasn't unhealthy. And that's what made it so hard to let go.

If she had been cruel, if we had outgrown each other, if we had been fighting endlessly—it would have been easier. But the hardest decisions in life aren't between good and bad. They're between good and good, where choosing one means losing the other.

In the end, I had to be honest with myself: I would be no good to her—or to any future family we might have—if I was living a life that felt like a compromise. What seems like self-sacrifice in the short term often turns into resentment in the long term. I knew that if I stayed, I would wake up years later feeling trapped, wondering what could have been, and that was unfair to both of us.

In Jewish mysticism, there is a teaching that sometimes the greatest love is the willingness to walk away. The Zohar describes love as a force that must be expansive—one that allows each person to fulfill their highest potential. Staying in a relationship at the cost of one's soul's growth is not love; it is attachment. True love, according to this teaching, is the courage to release someone when the path forward no longer aligns.

The weeks that followed were brutal. There were nights I questioned everything, moments when I doubted my decision, and stretches of time when I wanted nothing more than to turn back. But growth always requires pain.

Three things helped me move through the grief:

1. Understanding that endings don't negate the beauty of what was. Just because something ends doesn't mean it wasn't real, valuable, or meaningful. Some love stories are meant to shape us, not to stay with us forever.

2. Recognizing that our choices define our future. If I had stayed, I would have built a life from a place of fear—fear of being alone, fear of hurting someone I cared about. Leaving was a choice rooted in faith—faith that what was ahead would be worth the loss.

3. Trusting that what is meant for me will not require me to abandon myself. The right life, the right love, the right purpose—these things do not demand that we shrink. They expand us. And anything that requires us to sacrifice our deepest calling is not meant to be ours forever.

One of the greatest lessons I learned from this experience was that love does not mean ownership. So often, we believe that if we love something, we must hold onto it. But true love does not cling—it trusts.

Love, in its purest form, says: I honor who you are and where you need to go—even if that means letting you go.

Letting go of someone I loved was not a sign of weakness. It was an act of deep respect—for myself, for her, and for the life we both deserved to live.

And years later, as I look back, I do so with gratitude. Not because I didn't love her enough to stay, but because I loved both of us enough to let go.

How Letting Go Opened New Doors

There is a strange paradox in life—one that I resisted for years but have come to understand deeply: sometimes, holding on too tightly keeps us from receiving what is meant for us. We spend so much time gripping onto identities, careers, relationships, and dreams that we have outgrown, believing that letting go would mean losing everything. But what if, instead, it meant gaining something even greater?

For most of my adult life, I had built my identity meticulously. I was a creator, an entrepreneur, a thinker, and a man who pursued his goals with unwavering determination. I carefully constructed an image of myself based on success, resilience, and independence. But there was a problem: so much of this identity was built on external validation. The titles, the achievements, the recognition—I wore them like armor, believing they defined my worth.

Then, life did what it does best—it tore that identity apart.

The series of financial losses, professional setbacks, and personal crises I faced in a short period left me without the very things I thought made me me. My businesses crumbled, my financial security evaporated, and my sense of control was shattered. At first, I fought back, desperately trying to salvage the life I had built. I clung to what was slipping away, believing that if I just worked harder, strategized better, and refused to give in, I could rebuild what had been lost.

But what if it wasn't meant to be rebuilt? What if my old life had to fall apart to make way for something new?

Psychologists have long studied the phenomenon of identity foreclosure—a term describing individuals who become so attached to a particular identity that they resist change, even when it is necessary for their growth. We see this in professionals who stay in careers that no longer fulfill them, in relationships that have long ceased to nurture them, and in personal narratives that no longer align with who they have become.

Studies on post-traumatic growth suggest that individuals who endure profound life disruptions often emerge with a stronger, more flexible sense of self. When we let go of the rigid structures that once defined us, we create space for reinvention.

In neuroscience, research on neuroplasticity reveals that the brain is designed for change. The more we expose ourselves to new experiences, perspectives, and ways of being, the more adaptable and resilient we become. This means that even when it feels like we are losing everything, our brains are wired to rebuild and reimagine our reality.

For the first time in my life, I found myself without a clear title, without a stable business, and without a predictable plan. The version of myself I had spent years crafting had been stripped away. But instead of destruction, something unexpected happened:

I felt free.

The weight I had been carrying—the need to maintain an image, to chase a version of success that was no longer mine, to uphold an identity that had become suffocating—was gone. In its place was space. Space to explore. Space to ask new questions. Space to finally listen to the part of me that had been whispering all along: There is more.

This wasn't a loss. It was a rebirth.

Instead of forcing my way back into old structures, I surrendered to what was unfolding. And that's when things started to flow in ways I never could have predicted.

A publishing opportunity emerged—one that aligned far more with my purpose than my previous business ventures.

New connections were formed—relationships that were rooted in authenticity rather than status.

Creative projects that had once been hobbies took center stage, leading me down a path I hadn't even considered before.

None of this would have been possible had I kept holding onto what was.

In Kabbalah, there is a concept known as klipot—the shells that cover the divine spark within us. These shells represent the false narratives, attachments, and external layers that keep us disconnected from our true essence. The process of spiritual transformation involves breaking these shells, peeling back the layers of ego, expectation, and fear to reveal what is real and eternal within us.

This idea mirrors what I experienced. My old identity—built on achievements, external success, and societal definitions—was a shell. When it cracked, I wasn't left with nothing. I was left with truth.

The Zohar, the foundational text of Kabbalah, teaches:

"To reach higher levels of being, one must release the illusions of control. The hand that is full cannot receive."

This struck me deeply. I had spent so many years gripping onto what I thought I needed, never realizing that my clenched fists left no room to receive what life was trying to offer me. Only in letting go could I finally receive.

The experience of losing everything I once thought mattered taught me an entirely new definition of success:

Success is not a rigid plan. It is the ability to adapt.

Success is not external validation. It is internal alignment.

Success is not control. It is trust.

Looking back, I now see that every loss was, in reality, a gift. The ending of one chapter made space for another. The shedding of an old identity allowed for a more authentic self to emerge.

And perhaps, this is the secret of letting go: what we release was never truly ours to keep. It was only ever ours to experience, to learn from, and then to set free.

Spiritual or Psychological Shifts

There are moments in life when a single insight—whether through personal experience, therapy, or spiritual practice—has the power to shatter everything we once believed. These moments do not arrive gently. They often come in the wake of pain, loss, or relentless searching, forcing us to see reality through an entirely new lens.

For me, that moment came during my first spiritual retreat with Or HaLev at Big Bear, Southern California. Up until that point, I had approached spirituality as something to be understood intellectually, dissected, and analyzed. I had read countless books, explored different traditions, and attended religious gatherings. But knowledge alone had not been enough to fill the void I felt inside. I was searching for something deeper—something beyond words.

Then, in the stillness of that retreat, something broke open within me.

During a walk in the woods behind the cabin I was assigned to stay in, I suddenly felt an overwhelming flood of emotion. I fell to my knees and wept—not out of sadness, but out of a profound sense of recognition. It was as if, in that moment, I had been given the answer to a question I hadn't even known I was asking. A message, clear and undeniable, echoed within me:

"You have arrived."

It wasn't a voice. It wasn't an external revelation. It was something deeper—an internal knowing. I suddenly understood, in a way that defied logic, that everything I had gone through in my life—the highs, the deep lows, the heartbreaks, the losses—had been part of a meticulously woven journey. None of it had been accidental. None of it had been random.

I saw, with absolute clarity, that my life had been guided—not in the way I had once imagined, as a path of reward or punishment, but as a process of refinement. Every challenge had shaped me. Every fall had forced me to rise. Every loss had cleared space for something greater.

I wept for the version of myself that had resisted, that had fought against life rather than flowing with it. And in that moment of surrender, something within me shifted permanently.

Psychologists and neuroscientists have studied spiritual awakening and mystical experiences for decades, revealing fascinating insights about how profound realizations change the brain. Research shows that moments of deep spiritual insight activate the default mode network (DMN)—the system in the brain responsible for self-reflection and meaning-making. When individuals experience profound spiritual shifts, activity in the prefrontal cortex (the area associated with control and logical reasoning) decreases, while activity in the limbic system (the emotional and intuitive center) increases.

This suggests that true spiritual transformation isn't a process of thinking—it's a process of feeling, experiencing, and surrendering.

A study conducted by Andrew Newberg, a neuroscientist specializing in neurotheology, found that deep meditation and spiritual experiences alter brain structure, increasing the thickness of the posterior cingulate cortex—the region associated with self-awareness and emotional processing. This means that moments of surrender aren't just psychological shifts; they leave a lasting impact on our neurology, fundamentally changing the way we perceive ourselves and the world.

For me, that shift was undeniable. I walked into the retreat as someone searching for meaning. I walked out as someone who had found trust.

Kabbalah teaches that every soul is sent into the world with a tikun—a specific purpose for refinement and transformation. The Ari (Rabbi Isaac Luria) explained that every hardship, every moment of suffering, and every period of darkness is not a punishment, but a correction—a realignment of the soul with its true path.

The Baal Shem Tov, founder of Hasidic Judaism, expanded on this idea, teaching that everything we encounter in life is a conversation between us and the Divine. Every obstacle is an invitation. Every setback is a redirection.

This idea mirrored what I had experienced on the retreat. I had spent years believing that suffering was something to escape, something unfair or undeserved. But in that moment, I saw it differently: every hardship had been an initiation.

Kabbalah speaks of the Sefirot, the ten spiritual dimensions through which divine energy flows. The lowest of these, Malkhut (kingship), represents the physical world— the realm of struggle, ego, and separation. But Malkhut is not the end of the journey. It is the starting point. Through our struggles, we ascend. Through surrender, we elevate. Through trust, we transform.

In many spiritual traditions, the concept of ego death is seen as an essential part of awakening. Carl Jung, the renowned psychoanalyst, described this process as individuation—the integration of the unconscious and conscious self. In simple terms: the old self must dissolve for the true self to emerge.

This is exactly what I felt that day in Big Bear. The person I had been—the one who clung to certainty, who demanded answers, who sought validation from external success—died. And in its place, something new was born:

A person who no longer needed to know everything.

A person who could walk forward without controlling the path.

A person who understood, for the first time, that he was enough—just as he was.

Looking back, I realize that my greatest struggle had always been resistance. I resisted the unknown. I resisted hardship. I resisted any part of life that didn't conform to my plans. But in that moment of surrender, I saw that trust is the antidote to resistance.

We spend so much time trying to fix, predict, and control our lives. But what if everything is unfolding exactly as it should?

What if we are not lost?

What if we are being guided in ways we cannot yet see?

What if the things we fear are taking us exactly where we need to go?

There is a passage in the Talmud that says:

"Everything is in the hands of Heaven, except the fear of Heaven."

This means that our only true choice in life is not control—it is trust.

When I left that retreat, I was no longer asking, What's next?

I was simply saying, Thank you. Because I knew—I had arrived.

The Strength in Softness

Letting go is often mistaken for weakness. We are taught that strength means holding on, pushing forward, and never backing down. We admire resilience, perseverance, and the ability to endure. And yet, as I have learned through every stage of my life, the deepest kind of strength is not in resisting—it is in releasing.

To surrender is not to lose—it is to trust.

We live in a world that worships certainty. We want clear paths, defined identities, and guaranteed outcomes. But life is anything but predictable. It moves in rhythms we cannot control, unfolding in ways that often defy our expectations. And the more we try to force our way through, the more exhausted we become.

In my own journey, I have held on when I should have let go. I have fought battles that were never mine to fight. I have clung to beliefs that no longer served me, to identities that no longer fit, to relationships that had already run their course. And each time, I thought that letting go would break me.

But it never did.

Letting go didn't weaken me—it freed me.

Psychologists have long studied the paradox of strength, showing that true resilience is not in rigidity, but in adaptability. Research in emotional intelligence reveals that individuals who embrace flexibility—who are able to shift perspectives, release attachments, and adapt to changing circumstances—are significantly more resilient than those who cling rigidly to control.

This aligns with what Zen Buddhism teaches about the "unbendable arm." If you try to resist the force of a river, you will be overpowered. But if you learn to move with the current, you will never be broken.

Neuroscientific studies on psychological flexibility confirm that people who resist change experience heightened stress responses in the amygdala—the brain's fear center. But those who accept uncertainty show increased activity in the prefrontal cortex, which governs problem-solving, self-awareness, and long-term vision.

In other words, those who surrender are not weak—they are wise.

In Jewish mysticism, there is a profound concept called Bitul, which means self-nullification—not in the sense of erasing oneself, but in dissolving the ego's need to control. The Kabbalists teach that the greatest spiritual transformation happens not when we grip tightly to our own desires, but when we allow ourselves to be vessels for something greater.

This is mirrored in the principle of Ayin (nothingness). The sages teach that to reach enlightenment, one must pass through a state of Ayin—a space of surrender, where identity dissolves, and only divine presence remains.

What if the things we hold onto are the very things keeping us from expansion?

What if surrender is not about giving up, but about becoming something greater than we imagined?

The Tao Te Ching speaks of water as the most powerful force in nature—not because it is strong, but because it is soft.

"Nothing in the world is softer than water, yet nothing can wear away rock like it. The soft overcomes the hard, the gentle overcomes the rigid."

Softness does not mean fragility. It means fluidity. It means knowing when to release rather than resist, when to bend rather than break, when to trust rather than demand certainty.

Letting go is not an act of passivity—it is an act of profound courage. It is stepping into the unknown with open hands instead of clenched fists. It is choosing to flow with life rather than fight against it.

I do not claim to have mastered surrender. There are still moments when I find myself clinging—grasping for certainty, resisting change, fearing what I cannot control. But each time, I return to this truth:

The more I let go, the more life flows effortlessly.

Every major turning point in my life—from business failures to personal losses, from spiritual awakenings to unexpected opportunities—has come not from controlling, but from releasing.

So I ask you:

What are you holding onto that is holding you back?

What would happen if you released the need to know what comes next?

What if, instead of resisting, you trusted?

Because the truth is, we were never meant to control everything.

And in the letting go, we find the freedom we have been searching for all along.

Chapter 9: The Wisdom of Surrender

The Strength in Letting Go

When I moved to Los Angeles, I did something that went against everything I had ever known. For the first time in my life, I didn't prepare, I didn't plan, I didn't map out every step before making the leap. I just got in my car and drove. No job lined up. No apartment secured. No idea what would come next.

It was one of the most freeing moments of my life.

There was something about being fresh out of a spiritual retreat, having experienced a complete renewal of self, that made me open to the unknown in a way I had never been before. For years, I had lived under the weight of needing to control—my career, my finances, my relationships, even my own emotions. I had been conditioned to believe that security came from planning, that success was built on preparation, and that letting go was just another word for failure.

But this time, I didn't care about control. I didn't stress over the uncertainty. I didn't fear the unknown. I embraced it. And for the first time, I truly understood that surrender wasn't about weakness—it was the greatest act of strength I had ever experienced.

Within days of arriving in Los Angeles, everything started falling into place. I found an apartment with ease. I landed a retail job that covered my rent almost immediately. And the most surprising part? None of it felt like a struggle. It was as if life had simply been waiting for me to stop resisting, to step into the current rather than constantly trying to swim upstream.

Psychologists call this "cognitive ease"—a state in which the brain functions at its best when we are not caught in over-analysis or excessive resistance. Research suggests that our stress levels significantly decrease when we accept uncertainty rather than battle against it. Neuroscientist Richard Davidson has found that individuals who embrace change with a mindset of openness experience greater emotional resilience and even improved neural plasticity—the brain's ability to adapt and form new connections.

This is what surrender is. Not a passive resignation, but a conscious choice to trust the unfolding of life. A willingness to release the illusion that we must have everything figured out before we take the first step.

My journey to Los Angeles wasn't just a change in location—it was a transformation in the way I moved through the world. I wasn't running on fear. I wasn't weighed down by expectations. I was simply present, allowing life to happen instead of trying to force it into submission. And in doing so, I discovered something far more powerful than control: flow.

Surrender is not about giving up. It is about stepping into something greater than we ever could have imagined for ourselves.

Lessons from Nature or Everyday Life: The Wisdom of Flow

There is a reason we are drawn to nature when we seek peace. A walk by the ocean, the rustling of leaves in a quiet forest, the effortless way a river carves its path through the earth—nature is the greatest teacher of surrender. Unlike humans, nature does not resist what is. A tree does not fight the wind; it bends. A river does not battle the obstacles in its way; it flows around them.

I have always loved rivers for this reason. There is something deeply inspiring about their quiet persistence. They do not force their way through the landscape; they simply move forward, shaping the world as they go. A river never clings to the banks it has passed, nor does it resist the journey ahead. It trusts in the pull of gravity, in the natural course of things. It knows that forward is the only way.

During my transition to Los Angeles, I found myself reflecting on this idea constantly. I had spent most of my life trying to control my direction—planning, strategizing, ensuring that every step was accounted for. But in that moment, for the first time, I simply let go. I allowed myself to flow like the river, trusting that wherever life carried me was exactly where I needed to be. And just as a river never questions its path, I chose to stop questioning mine.

This idea is not just poetic; it is deeply rooted in psychology and philosophy. The concept of "flow", as introduced by Mihaly Csikszentmihalyi, describes the state of complete immersion in an experience, where action and awareness merge effortlessly. Studies show that people who achieve flow state experience greater happiness, creativity, and overall well-being. Interestingly, flow is not achieved through control but through surrender—by being fully present and allowing life to unfold naturally.

In Taoist philosophy, this is known as Wu Wei—"effortless action" or "action without force." The Tao Te Ching, an ancient Chinese text, teaches that the wisest way to navigate life is not by forcing outcomes but by aligning with the natural rhythm of things. Lao Tzu, the father of Taoism, put it simply:

"Be like water, which is soft and yielding, yet overcomes the hardest of obstacles."

Water does not resist—it adapts. It finds a way forward without struggle.

Modern neuroscience supports this wisdom. Studies on cognitive flexibility reveal that people who embrace adaptability, rather than rigid control, are more resilient in the face of change. The brain thrives when it is open to possibilities, rather than fixated on a single path. Resistance, in contrast, activates the brain's stress response, flooding the body with cortisol and narrowing our ability to see solutions.

This lesson—of moving like water, of embracing flow—has shaped the way I now approach life. It is not about passivity, nor is it about giving up. It is about trusting that there is an intelligence beyond our immediate understanding, a current beneath the surface that knows where we are meant to go. When we let go of resistance, we allow ourselves to be carried to places we never could have reached by force alone.

Looking back, I see that every time I let go, life carried me somewhere better than I had imagined. And every time I resisted, I exhausted myself fighting against what was always meant to be. The river does not worry about where it will end up. It simply flows.

And maybe—just maybe—that is the real secret to peace.

Spiritual or Philosophical Perspectives: A New Understanding of Surrender

There are books we read, and then there are books that read us. The Untethered Soul by Michael A. Singer was one of those books for me. It didn't just offer new information—it unraveled old beliefs. It challenged the way I had structured my life around control, around self-definition, around the identity I had spent decades constructing. And, perhaps most profoundly, it introduced me to the idea that

surrender is not just a single act but an ongoing way of living.

Singer's core message is simple yet radical: the key to inner freedom lies in letting go of the voice in our heads that
constantly clings, resists, and demands control. This voice,
the ceaseless inner dialogue that narrates our lives, is the
source of much of our suffering. We mistake it for our true
self, but in reality, it is just conditioned thought—a collec-
tion of fears, past wounds, and learned behaviors mas-
querading as identity.

For years, I had believed that my thoughts and emotions
defined me. If I felt insecure, I was insecure. If I felt unworthy, I was unworthy. I had built my entire sense of self
around internal dialogue, around stories I had inherited
and reinforced over time. But The Untethered Soul made
me question: What if I am not that voice? What if the real
me is the one observing that voice—the silent awareness
behind it?

This shift in perspective was more than intellectual; it was
experiential. As I practiced what Singer described—observing my thoughts rather than identifying with them—I
noticed something remarkable. The thoughts that once
ruled me lost their power. They still appeared, but they no
longer dictated my actions. I could let them pass, like
clouds drifting across the sky, without grasping at them or
fighting them.

For the first time, I understood surrender as something
deeper than simply "letting go" of a situation. It was about
letting go of myself—at least, the false self I had spent so
much time defending. It was about loosening my grip on
identity, expectations, and the need to control my emotions
or the world around me.

This idea of stepping back from our thoughts and emotions
is not unique to Singer. It echoes across spiritual traditions.
In Buddhism, the concept of non-attachment teaches that

suffering comes from clinging—whether to ideas, possessions, or identities. The more we hold on, the more we struggle. The Taoist philosophy of wu wei (effortless action) similarly encourages flowing with life rather than resisting it, trusting that things will unfold as they should.

In Kabbalah, there is a concept known as bitul ha'yesh, or the nullification of the self. It teaches that the more we cling to a rigid sense of "I," the more we block divine flow. True surrender is not passivity; it is an opening—a willingness to let the higher order of life move through us rather than trying to force our own will onto reality.

At first, this idea was terrifying. If I wasn't my thoughts, my fears, my ambitions—then what was I? The ego resists surrender because it fears obliteration. It tells us that if we let go, we will cease to exist. But the paradox is that true surrender doesn't erase us—it frees us. What disappears is not the self, but the suffering we mistakenly believed was part of it.

I began to practice this surrender in everyday moments. When an old fear arose, instead of engaging with it, I let it be. When a situation didn't go as planned, I stopped trying to control it. When someone disappointed me, I released the expectation that they should have acted differently. Each time, I felt lighter. Not in a detached, numb way, but in a profoundly peaceful way.

Letting go didn't mean I stopped caring. It meant I stopped clinging.

I had spent so much of my life believing that control equaled strength. That to be powerful was to hold on—to ideas, to plans, to my sense of self. But The Untethered Soul showed me that real power is in the opposite direction. The strongest thing we can do is release the weight we were never meant to carry.

Through this surrender, I found something I never expected: clarity. The more I let go, the more life revealed itself. Opportunities arose without struggle. Answers surfaced without force. And most importantly, I felt a deep, unshakable sense of trust—not in specific outcomes, but in the unfolding of life itself.

Surrender is not a single moment of letting go; it is a lifelong practice. And the more we practice, the freer we become.

The Final Surrender: Letting Go Completely

There is a moment in every journey of surrender where we realize that we are no longer just letting go of small attachments, passing fears, or transient desires. We are letting go of the need to control anything at all.

At first, this idea seems impossible. Our entire lives, we are conditioned to believe that control is necessary—that without it, we will fall apart. We are taught to set goals, plan for the future, anticipate risks, and build safety nets. And for most of life, this approach seems logical. It helps us survive, achieve, and maintain a sense of order.

But what happens when we reach a point where control no longer serves us? When we realize that, no matter how much we try, we cannot force life to conform to our plans? What happens when surrender is not just a choice but the only way forward?

For me, that moment came when I finally understood that surrender was not about trusting a specific outcome—it was about trusting life itself. It was about releasing the illusion that I was the architect of everything, that my effort alone determined what would happen next.

The greatest resistance to surrender is fear. It whispers to us:

"If I let go, will everything fall apart?"

"If I stop trying to control, will I be left with nothing?"

"If I trust, what if life doesn't catch me?"

This fear is deeply rooted in our biology. The human brain is wired for survival, and control gives us a sense of security. Neuroscientific studies have shown that uncertainty triggers the amygdala—the brain's fear center—activating stress responses similar to those experienced in life-threatening situations. This is why surrender feels so difficult. It feels like stepping off a cliff, trusting that something unseen will hold us.

But what if the very thing we fear—falling—is actually the way we learn to fly?

Spiritual traditions across cultures have long emphasized this paradox. The Tao Te Ching teaches:

"When you let go of what you are, you become what you might be."

In Buddhism, there is a teaching that the tighter we cling, the more we suffer. The moment we release our grip, we don't lose control—we gain freedom.

In Jewish mysticism, the idea of Ayin—a state of nothingness—is considered the gateway to divine wisdom. The Kabbalists teach that true enlightenment is found not in accumulating more knowledge, but in emptying ourselves of attachment. To step into Ayin is to trust that in our emptiness, something greater will arise.

I once believed that surrender was passive. That it meant giving up. But I have come to see that surrender is the bravest thing a person can do. It is the act of stepping into the unknown with open hands, saying, "I no longer need to control this. I trust that whatever comes will be exactly what is meant for me."

There was a moment, sitting in that forest in Big Bear, when I finally let go completely. I wasn't thinking about the past or planning the future. I wasn't trying to fix anything, achieve anything, or prove anything. I simply was.

For the first time, I felt the vastness of life—not as something to manage, but as something to experience.

And in that moment, I understood:

I never had control.

I never needed it.

Life had always been carrying me.

From that day forward, I no longer measured my success by what I could control. I measured it by how open I was— how willing I was to let life flow through me instead of trying to shape it into what I thought it should be.

This does not mean I stopped making decisions, setting goals, or taking action. But I now move through life with a different energy. Instead of gripping tightly, I hold things lightly. Instead of fearing change, I welcome it. Instead of resisting what comes, I trust that it is here to teach me something.

To surrender completely is not to stop living—it is to start living fully.

It is to wake up each day with curiosity instead of expectation.

It is to embrace uncertainty as a doorway rather than a threat.

It is to replace fear with faith—not faith in a specific outcome, but faith in the journey itself.

And in this final surrender, we find the thing we have been searching for all along: peace.

Because the truth is, we were never meant to control it all.

We were meant to experience it.

The Journey Continues

Surrender is not a one-time decision. It is a practice. It is a way of being. And the more we embrace it, the freer we become.

Letting go is not the end of our power—it is the beginning of something far greater.

It is the doorway to a life lived in flow, trust, and deep, unshakable peace.

Because when we finally stop trying to hold everything together, we realize...

Everything was never falling apart. It was falling into place.

Chapter 10: The Wisdom of Letting Go

We've spent this entire journey exploring the art of surrender—its power, its challenges, and its necessity. And now, we arrive at the final chapter, where we step beyond lessons and into the lived experience of letting go. This is not a conclusion, but an opening. A threshold. Because letting go is not something we do once—it is something we must learn to embody, over and over again.

To let go is to understand that life is not asking us to hold on, but to participate. To engage, to experience, to love, to lose, to begin again. Over the years, I have come to see that surrender is not about retreating—it is about stepping forward without resistance. It is about being fully present in a world that is constantly changing, fully alive in a body that is always aging, fully committed to a life that is, by its very nature, fleeting.

The Final Layer of Letting Go: The Illusion of Control

One of the greatest paradoxes of life is that the more we try to control it, the more it controls us. The ancient Stoics understood this well. Epictetus taught:

"Some things are up to us, and some things are not. If you desire what is beyond your control, you will be disturbed; but if you only desire what is within your power, you will be free."

The hardest lesson I had to learn was this: most of what I thought I could control was an illusion. I couldn't control whether people stayed or left, whether opportunities materialized or dissolved, whether my body remained strong or faltered with time. I spent years fighting against reality, believing that if I could just anticipate every obstacle, outwork every uncertainty, and overprepare for every possibility, I could secure myself against suffering.

But suffering came anyway.

Not as a punishment, but as a teacher.

Suffering showed me that my control was never real. And once I stopped resisting, once I stopped demanding that life conform to my plans, something unexpected happened—I discovered peace. Not because life became easier, but because I stopped expecting it to be anything other than what it was.

This is the wisdom of letting go. Not to abandon effort, not to relinquish responsibility, but to release the need for life to unfold on our terms.

The river does not stop flowing because a rock stands in its way. It moves around it, reshaping the landscape as it goes. We are meant to do the same.

The Beauty of Unfinished Stories

We often resist letting go because we want closure. We want guarantees. We want to know how the story ends. But life rarely gives us neat endings. Sometimes, the people who leave our lives never come back. The dreams we once held so tightly never materialize. The apologies we long for never arrive.

And yet, life goes on.

In Japanese aesthetics, there is a concept called wabi-sabi, the acceptance of imperfection and incompleteness. It is the understanding that beauty is found in things that are unfinished, fleeting, and imperfect. A cracked bowl, mended with gold. A cherry blossom, blooming for only a moment before falling. A story, left without an ending.

We, too, are unfinished. Our lives are not meant to be neatly resolved, but to be lived fully, even in uncertainty.

I used to believe that the goal was to reach a point where everything finally made sense. But I have come to see that true wisdom is the ability to live without needing all the answers. To be at peace in the midst of the unknown. To trust the unfolding.

A Life Without Holding On

What would it look like to live without grasping? Without clinging to what is already slipping through our fingers? What if, instead of fighting for certainty, we welcomed the unknown as an old friend?

The great Persian poet Rumi wrote:

"Try not to resist the changes that come your way. Instead, let life live through you."

This is the final lesson of letting go—not to see surrender as a loss, but as the ultimate act of trust. Trust that we are being carried, even when we cannot see the current. Trust that endings are also beginnings. Trust that life is not something we must conquer, but something we are meant to experience.

If there is one thing I hope you take from this book, it is this: your peace is not in control, but in trust.

Trust that you are exactly where you are meant to be.

Trust that what is meant for you will find its way to you.

Trust that you do not need to force, chase, or hold on to anything for dear life.

Trust that letting go is not falling—it is flying.

The Closing of One Chapter, the Opening of Another

This book does not end here, because surrender is not an ending—it is a way of being. It is an ongoing practice, a choice we must make each day.

Some days, letting go will feel effortless. Other days, it will feel like the hardest thing in the world. But each time you choose surrender, you choose freedom.

You choose to stop fighting against life and instead walk with it.

And that is the greatest act of strength there is.

Bibliography

A

- Alloy, L. B., & Abramson, L. Y. (1979). *Judgment of contingency in depressed and nondepressed students: Sadder but wiser? Journal of Experimental Psychology: General, 108(4)*, 441–485.
- Amabile, T. M., & Pratt, M. G. (2016). *The Dynamic Componential Model of Creativity and Innovation in Organizations. Creativity Research Journal.*
- American Psychological Association (APA). (2020). *Stress in America: The Impact of Control and Burnout in High Achievers.*
- Barlow, D. H. (2002). *Anxiety and Its Disorders: The Nature and Treatment of Anxiety and Panic.* Guilford Press.
- Baal Shem Tov. *Collected Teachings on Divine Timing and Trust.*
- Baal Shem Tov (1700-1760). *Teachings on Hashgacha Pratit (Divine Providence), collected in Tzava'at HaRivash.*
- Bach, D. R., & Dolan, R. J. (2012). *Knowing how much you don't know: A neural organization of un-*

certainty estimates. Nature Neuroscience, 15(10),
1465–1470.

- Beaty, R. E., Benedek, M., Silvia, P. J., & Schacter, D. L. (2018). *Creative Cognition and the Brain's Default Network: A Review and Theoretical Framework. Neuropsychologia, 118,* 48-56.

- Bonanno, G. A. (2004). *Loss, Trauma, and Human Resilience: Have We Underestimated the Human Capacity to Thrive After Extremely Aversive Events? American Psychologist, 59(1),* 20–28.

- Bowlby, J. (1988). *A Secure Base: Parent-Child Attachment and Healthy Human Development.* Basic Books.

- Briere, J., & Scott, C. (2014). *Principles of Trauma Therapy: A Guide to Symptoms, Evaluation, and Treatment.* Sage Publications.

- Brewer, J. A., Worhunsky, P. D., Gray, J. R., Tang, Y.-Y., Weber, J., & Kober, H. (2011). *Meditation Experience Is Associated with Differences in Default Mode Network Activity and Connectivity. Proceedings of the National Academy of Sciences, 108(50),* 20254–20259.

- Brown, B. (2012). *Daring Greatly: How the Courage to Be Vulnerable Transforms the Way We Live, Love, Parent, and Lead.* Penguin Random House.

C

- Canevello, A., & Crocker, J. (2011). *Interpersonal Goals and Relationships: The Costs of Control-Oriented Motivations. Journal of Social and Personal Relationships.*
- Carstensen, L. L. (2006). *The Influence of a Sense of Time on Human Development. Science, 312(5782),* 1913–1915.
- Carver, C. S., Scheier, M. F., & Segerstrom, S. C. (2010). *Optimism. Clinical Psychology Review, 30(7),* 879–889.
- Csikszentmihalyi, M. (1990). *Flow: The Psychology of Optimal Experience.* Harper & Row.
- Curran, T., & Hill, A. P. (2019). *The Rise of Perfectionism: A Study on Cultural and Generational Trends.*

D

- Deci, E. L., & Ryan, R. M. (1985). *Self-Determination Theory: The Psychological Impact of Control.*
- Dietrich, A. (2004). *The Cognitive Neuroscience of Creativity. Psychonomic Bulletin & Review, 11(6),* 1011–1026.

- Duffy, M. K., & Flett, G. L. (2016). *The Role of Perfectionism in Workplace Productivity and Well-Being. Harvard Business Review.*

E

- Edison, T. A. (1914). *Fire at Edison's Laboratory. The New York Times.*
- Edmondson, A. C. (2019). *The Fearless Organization: Creating Psychological Safety in the Workplace for Learning, Innovation, and Growth.* Harvard Business Review Press.
- Epictetus. *The Discourses.* Trans. Robin Hard. Oxford University Press.
- Epstude, K., & Roese, N. J. (2008). *The Functional Theory of Counterfactual Thinking. Personality and Social Psychology Review, 12(2),* 168–192.

F

- Festinger, L. (1954). *A Theory of Social Comparison Processes. Human Relations.*
- Flett, G. L., Hewitt, P. L., & Cheng, W. (2002). *Perfectionism and Its Impact on Self-Esteem in Adulthood.*
- Fox, J., & Moreland, J. J. (2015). *The Dark Side of Social Networking Sites: An Exploration of the Re-*

lational and Psychological Effects of Facebook. Computers in Human Behavior.

G

- Garland, E. L., Farb, N. A., Goldin, P. R., & Fredrickson, B. L. (2015). *The Mindfulness-to-Meaning Theory: Extensions, Applications, and Future Directions. Psychological Inquiry.*
- Gilbert, E. (2006). *Eat, Pray, Love: One Woman's Search for Everything Across Italy, India, and Indonesia.* Penguin Books.
- Gottman, J. M., & Silver, N. (1999). *The Seven Principles for Making Marriage Work.* Harmony Books.

H

- Hayes, S. C., Strosahl, K. D., & Wilson, K. G. (2006). *Acceptance and Commitment Therapy: An Experiential Approach to Behavior Change.*
- Hirsh, J. B., Mar, R. A., & Peterson, J. B. (2012). *Psychological Entropy: A Framework for Understanding Uncertainty-Related Anxiety. Psychological Review, 119(2),* 304–320.

K

- Kabat-Zinn, J. (1990). *Full Catastrophe Living: Using the Wisdom of Your Body and Mind to Face Stress, Pain, and Illness.* Delacorte Press.
- Kabat-Zinn, J. (2003). *Mindfulness-Based Interventions in Context: Past, Present, and Future. Clinical Psychology: Science and Practice.*
- Kashdan, T. B., & Rottenberg, J. (2010). *Psychological Flexibility as a Fundamental Aspect of Health. Clinical Psychology Review, 30(7),* 865–878.
- Koppe, G., Jarecki, J., & Brosowski, T. (2021). *The Paradox of Control: Why High Control-Seeking Behavior Leads to Increased Anxiety and Burnout. Journal of Anxiety Disorders, 45(3),* 17-32.

L

- Laozi. *Tao Te Ching.* Trans. Stephen Mitchell. Harper Perennial Modern Classics.
- Langer, E. J. (1975). *The Illusion of Control. Journal of Personality and Social Psychology, 32(2),* 311–328.
- Lomas, T., & Ivtzan, I. (2016). *Second Wave Positive Psychology: Exploring the Positive Benefits of*

Acceptance and Letting Go. Journal of Positive Psychology.

M

- Mandela, N. (1994). *Long Walk to Freedom: The Autobiography of Nelson Mandela.* Little, Brown and Company.
- Maslach, C., & Leiter, M. P. (2019). *Burnout: A Global Issue in the Workplace. World Health Organization Report.*
- Merton, R. K., & Barber, E. G. (2004). *The Travels and Adventures of Serendipity: A Study in Sociological Semantics and the Sociology of Science.* Princeton University Press.

R

- Rogers, C. R. (1961). *On Becoming a Person: A Therapist's View of Psychotherapy.* Houghton Mifflin Harcourt.
- Rumi. *The Essential Rumi.* Trans. Coleman Barks. HarperOne.
- Ryan, R. M., & Deci, E. L. (2000). *Self-Determination Theory and the Facilitation of Intrinsic Motivation, Social Development, and Well-Being. American Psychologist.*

S

- Sahdra, B., et al. (2010). *Control and Its Emotional Costs: A Study on Anxiety and Burnout.*
- Sapolsky, R. M. (2004). *Why Zebras Don't Get Ulcers.* New York: Henry Holt and Company.
- Schneider, B., et al. (2001). *Overestimating Influence and Its Psychological Costs: A Behavioral Study.*
- Schultz, W. (1998). *Predictive Reward Signal of Dopamine Neurons. Journal of Neurophysiology.*
- Seligman, M. E. P. (1991). *Learned Optimism: How to Change Your Mind and Your Life.*
- Singer, M. A. (2007). *The Untethered Soul: The Journey Beyond Yourself.* New Harbinger Publications.
- Smith, R., et al. (2021). *Perfectionism and Workplace Burnout: A Meta-Analysis.*

T

- Tang, Y. Y., Hölzel, B. K., & Posner, M. I. (2015). *The Neuroscience of Mindfulness Meditation. Nature Reviews Neuroscience.*
- Taylor, S. E., & Brown, J. D. (1988). *Illusion and Well-Being: A Social Psychological Perspective on Mental Health. Psychological Bulletin.*

- Tedeschi, R. G., & Calhoun, L. G. (2004). *Posttraumatic Growth: Conceptual Foundations and Empirical Evidence. Psychological Inquiry, 15(1), 1–18.*
- Twenge, J. M., & Martin, G. N. (2020). *Social Media Use and Its Impact on Perfectionism and Mental Health. Journal of Social and Clinical Psychology.*

V

- van der Kolk, B. (2014). *The Body Keeps the Score: Brain, Mind, and Body in the Healing of Trauma.* Penguin Books.

W

- Wegner, D. M. (2002). *The Illusion of Conscious Will.*
- Williams, R., et al. (2020). *Stress and Control: The Neurological Costs of Resistance.*

Z

- Zohar (2:262b). *The Hidden Light and the Nature of Delays in Spiritual Growth.*

About the Author

Ethan Starke is a writer, entrepreneur, and creative force whose career spans media, business, and personal transformation. With a background in film, television, and strategic leadership, he has spent decades navigating industries across continents, building companies, and experiencing firsthand the cycles of success, failure, and reinvention.

Ethan's storytelling journey began with a bestselling sci-fi trilogy, which opened doors to the world of filmmaking and global entrepreneurship. But it was his personal trials—the losses that forced him to surrender, the rebuilding that followed—that shaped his deepest insights. *The Science of Letting Go* is not just a book; it is the culmination of a lifetime spent learning when to fight, when to release, and how to trust the unseen forces that shape our lives.

Beyond this work, Ethan continues to explore themes of human connection, reinvention, and creative fulfillment. His book series *Curate a Date* helps couples break free from routine and rediscover joy in shared experiences. His podcast, *The Reel Debrief*, blends cinematic critique with deeper discussions about storytelling, culture, and artistic expression. His magazine, *The Starke Perspective*, and his podcasts, *Starke Conversations* and *The Starke Vision*, serves as platforms for thought leadership, personal growth, and reflections on the intersection of business, creativity, and philosophy.

Ethan's work—whether in writing, media, or entrepreneurship—is driven by the belief that transformation begins with courage: the courage to let go, to embrace change, and to step into the unknown.

For more on Ethan's work, including his books, essays, and projects, visit www.ethanstarke.com